Inside City Tourism

ASPECTS OF TOURISM
Series Editors: Chris Cooper, *Oxford Brookes University, UK*, C. Michael Hall, *University of Canterbury, New Zealand* and Dallen J. Timothy, *Arizona State University, USA*

Aspects of Tourism is an innovative, multifaceted series, which comprises authoritative reference handbooks on global tourism regions, research volumes, texts and monographs. It is designed to provide readers with the latest thinking on tourism worldwide and push back the frontiers of tourism knowledge. The volumes are authoritative, readable and user-friendly, providing accessible sources for further research. Books in the series are commissioned to probe the relationship between tourism and cognate subject areas such as strategy, development, retailing, sport and environmental studies.

Full details of all the books in this series and of all our other publications can be found on http://www.channelviewpublications.com, or by writing to Channel View Publications, St Nicholas House, 31–34 High Street, Bristol BS1 2AW, UK.

ASPECTS OF TOURISM
Series Editors: Chris Cooper, C. Michael Hall and Dallen J. Timothy

Inside City Tourism
A European Perspective

John Heeley

CHANNEL VIEW PUBLICATIONS
Bristol • Buffalo • Toronto

To my late Mum and Dad

Library of Congress Cataloging in Publication Data
A catalog record for this book is available from the Library of Congress.
Heeley, John, 1951-
Inside City Tourism: A European Perspective/John Heeley.
Aspects of Tourism
Includes bibliographical references.
1. Tourism--Europe. 2. Cities and towns--Europe. I. Title.
G155.E8H44 2011
338.4'7914–dc22 2011000632

British Library Cataloguing in Publication Data
A catalogue entry for this book is available from the British Library.

ISBN-13: 978-1-84541-171-8 (hbk)
ISBN-13: 978-1-84541-170-1 (pbk)

Channel View Publications
UK: St Nicholas House, 31–34 High Street, Bristol, BS1 2AW, UK.
USA: UTP, 2250 Military Road, Tonawanda, NY 14150, USA.
Canada: UTP, 5201 Dufferin Street, North York, Ontario M3H 5T8, Canada.

The policy of Multilingual Matters/Channel View Publications is to use papers that are natural, renewable and recyclable products, made from wood grown in sustainable forests. In the manufacturing process of our books, and to further support our policy, preference is given to printers that have FSC and PEFC Chain of Custody certification. The FSC and/or PEFC logos will appear on those books where full certification has been granted to the printer concerned.

Typeset by Techset Composition Ltd, Salisbury, UK.
Printed and bound in Great Britain by the MPG Books Group.

Contents

List of Figures and Tables

Figures

Tables

Acknowledgements

A great debt of gratitude is owed to all my colleagues and friends in European Cities Marketing without whom the European perspective of this book would have literally been impossible.

The book would have been equally impossible without a 40-year long career as tourism academic turned city marketer, so that there are further obligations to record. The former tourist chiefs of Glasgow and Gothenburg, Eddie Friel and Claes Bjerkne respectively, have been important sources of confidence and inspiration. Two businessmen were unfailingly generous and understanding; Don Lyon under whose tutelage at Sheffield I learned the 'basics' of how to be a chief executive; and John Saunders who at Nottingham endeavoured in the nicest possible way to 'round me off' as a CEO. Also in Sheffield there was the late Councillor Peter Horton, a wise and kind man from whom I developed an understanding of the politics, culture and arcane administrative routines of local government. Professor David Airey and I have been fellow travellers in tourism since 1972 and we continue to walk together and exchange information, ideas and gossip. A heartfelt word of thanks is also due to the bevy of talented and hard working professionals who supported me during my 19 years as a city marketing CEO, and in particular those personal assistants who were my right, and sometimes left, hands.

In preparing this book, I wish to credit Wolfgang Kraus, Gillian Cruddas and her team at Visit York, and Bart van de Velde for their help with Chapters 4, 6 and 8, respectively.

The final acknowledgement is to my wife Alison and son Stephen who have assisted in all manner of practical ways with the writing of this book. Suffice to say, responsibility for content is all mine.

John Heeley
July 2010

Two roads diverged in a wood, and I –
I took the one less travelled by,
And that has made all the difference.

Robert Frost

Preface: Why a Book on City Tourism?

I have spent 19 years of my working life in city tourism (1990–2009), and in that time set up 'from scratch' four city marketing agencies and then consolidated their ongoing development. It began with Sheffield (1990–1996) and Destination Sheffield, and there followed Coventry (1997–2001) and Coventry and Warwickshire Promotions, Birmingham (2001–2003) and Marketing Birmingham, and finally Nottingham and Experience Nottinghamshire (2003–2009). Prior to that, I had been an academic specialising in tourism at Strathclyde University, Glasgow (1978–1990). While lecturing there, I had been especially struck by how Glasgow was seeking to revive its economy, boldly using tourism to create new spending and jobs and to raise the city's profile. The substantive focus of this book – albeit from a pan European perspective – is the city tourism I studied in Glasgow and subsequently 'practised' as the creator and founder chief executive officer (CEO) of the four aforementioned city marketing agencies.

After over 40 years as a tourism researcher, academic, practitioner and consultant/writer, it is my considered view that the fundamental way in which cities market themselves effectively in early 21st century Europe is through the attraction and servicing of tourists. To be sure, there are forms of urban marketing taking place alongside that which targets tourists. Universities and colleges compete for prospective students and a part of their marketing activity focuses on the advantages of the city as opposed to the various courses and other on-site amenities. The same is true of promotional activities undertaken by local government designed to reinforce 'sense of place' amongst residents (the old-fashioned term was 'civic pride' and the new ones are 'place making' and 'place shaping'). Likewise with local government inward investment campaigns aiming to persuade companies and other occupiers of property to locate themselves in their particular city. Organisations representing the professional services sector also unite from time to time to promote their city's prowess as a hub of law, accountancy and property development, and similarly 'the sell' here emphasises at least in part the wider city offer.

Notwithstanding these and other manifestations of city marketing, I reiterate my conviction that at the core of effective city marketing lies the activities undertaken by city tourism organisation, especially when these are discharged alongside an overarching city branding campaign – as discussed in Chapters 7 and 8 of this book. It was during my tenure at Glasgow as an academic, studying and reflecting upon the role of the local tourist board there, that the following realisation struck home: if a city gets its tourism marketing right, attracting the leisure visitor and the conference delegate in what are surely the most competitive of all market places, then the infrastructure for just about everything else is more or less likely to be in place – be it good environment, accessibility, 'evening economy', shopping, resident 'feel good', prowess as a business centre or winning 'footloose' inward investors and students. Glasgow served as a laboratory, enabling me to witness firsthand the transformational effect on city image and reputation occasioned by tourists coming, seeing, liking and then telling numerous friends and relatives that the city was indeed (like Glasgow's slogan said at the time) 'miles better'. To be sure, the tourists injected money into the place directly – I liken tourism to a helicopter flying over the city dropping pound notes – but of even greater significance was this 'street level' repositioning of attitudes and perceptions, with all its positive 'knock on' effects for inward investment, civic pride, business development, attraction and retention of students and, of course, further tourism.

The motivation to now put pen to paper is sixfold.

First and of least importance, there is my own passion for cities, particularly for the one in which I was born and brought up, and in which I still to this day live – the northern English city of Sheffield. Cities creep under your skin and take a hold of you. As Kafka said of Prague 'This little mother has claws'. Another writer, Donleavy, eulogised Ireland's capital saying 'When I die I want to decompose in a barrel of porter and have it served in all the pubs in Dublin'. I would not go as far as this, but there is no denying the hold that can be exerted by cities (and for the author by one city in particular). As the politician and writer Roy Hattersley (1978) said 'Oscar Wilde believed that "when good Americans die, they go to Paris". There is no doubt where good Sheffielders go. They go to Sheffield'.

Secondly, during the 20 years I worked as a city marketer a remarkable paradigm shift occurred. From the mid-1990s onwards one way of seeing and making sense of the job – based on print, letters, pens, overhead projectors and heavy, unwieldy desk phones – gave way to another. Fifteen years ago there was no email, Google, iPod, generation Y, PowerPoint, social media, user-generated content, blogging, mobile phones with multimedia access and video footage, netbooks, CTR (click through rates), Facebook, Trip Advisor, viral marketing, interactive news releases and web 2.0.

Nowadays, internet and web activity with all their attendant trappings and paraphernalia are the medium through which the art and science of city tourism is practised. This quite fundamental transformation has occurred in what is historically a relatively short space of time – some 15 or so years is not a long time – and such a paradigm shift in tourism is something which I felt was important to 'bottle' and convey in writing.

Indeed, it may well be that we are currently on the cusp of a paradigm within a paradigm shift in respect of social media, and how it is lately being used in city marketing. From Reykjavik to Valencia, and with precious little strategy or criteria of success, city tourism and marketing organisations have, over the past two years, begun experimenting with social media: pages have been opened on Facebook, Twitter and Flikr; YouTube presences have been fastidiously developed; websites have been overhauled to incorporate multimedia; and partnerships have been struck with Trip Advisor, Google and others. Moreover, a handful of city marketing organisations, in a quintessentially 'learning by doing' fashion, have begun to use social media as an integral component of mainstream marketing campaigns. In such campaigns, social media is used alongside 'traditional' advertising and mailing activities. A good example is a short break campaign being undertaken this year by the Stockholm Visitors Board in conjunction with the national tourist organisation (Visit Sweden) and the Scandic Hotels group. The campaign addresses the neighbouring Norwegian and Danish markets, cleverly playing on Sweden's 'big brother' reputation in these two countries; one advertising image, for instance, shows a speed boat excursion set against a stunning Stockholm backdrop with the caption: 'Real Vikings come from Denmark of course, but we volunteer to act as your shipmates'. A campaign website offers advice on things to see and do in the Swedish capital, as well as a direct bookings link to Scandic Hotels. To drive traffic to this site, a combination of advertising mediums are called into play, majoring on the use of social media, but supplemented by advertising on Google, Facebook itself and outdoor posters. Uses of social media, for instance, include a 'flatter chart' on Facebook which seeks out Swedes willing to act as ambassadors of their country by persuading their Danish and Norwegian friends to take advantage of the short breaks on offer. Another Scandinavian city tourist organisation, Wonderful Copenhagen, is using Facebook to drive visits to its portal website, and is then measuring the conversion rate in terms of bookings. Also this year, the Vienna Tourist Board began to target bloggers as part of its media relations activities, and at the time of writing was developing an integrated social media strategy.

Using social media in these and other ways transforms the manner in which city tourist and marketing organisations communicate with their various audiences; the process becomes 'two way' and 'bottom up', as opposed to 'one way' and 'top down'. Over the next decade, the author anticipates a paradigm within a paradigm shift occurring in which social media will come to dominate the manner in which city tourist and marketing organisations reach and interact with their audiences. All of which seems light years away from the summer of 1990 and the pen, pad and burgundy leather briefcase with which I commenced my city marketing career as Director of Tourism for the City of Sheffield.

A third aspect I felt it important to reflect in the book is the debate and practice centred on the issues of tourism's sustainability. As a tourism researcher and academic in the 1970s and 1980s, I became aware of tourism's potential to 'kill the goose that lays the golden egg'; the very environments, cultures and host communities on which tourism depended were at one and the same time threatened by it. Cities such as Oxford and Venice were by then already capitulating in the face of mass tourism, and in the early 21st century reference is being made to the 'de-marketing' of such places (Coccossis & Mexa, 2004).

Albeit in a rural as opposed to urban context, the poet Wordsworth embodies the issues and paradoxes raised by tourism and sustainability. On his return to the Lake District from France in 1799 he was 'much disgusted' by the tourism developments that had occurred during his absence. He famously led a partially successful campaign in the 1840s which resisted the 'opening up' of the Lake District to rail borne tourists (Heeley, 1989). In letters and sonnets to the local newspaper, he opined that the beauty of Lakeland would be spoiled by the railway line itself and by all the development that would follow in its wake. He implored 'Is there then no nook of English ground secure from rash assault?' (de Selincourt, 1981). Wordsworth's entreaty was as much social and economic as it was environmental. He considered that only 'persons of taste and feeling' could properly appreciate the Lakes, and that meant well-to-do incomers like himself and the rich upper class travellers who visited the area each year. When the railway eventually came in 1847, the contradictions and tensions became ever more acute. Though on the side of the 'common man', Wordsworth did not wish to share with him his beloved lakes, hills and dales. Moreover, Wordsworth profited from the very 'opening up' of the Lakes that he had so steadfastly campaigned against. The sales of his erudite tourist guidebook multiplied, earning him more money from this source than from the poetry which represented his life's work (Davies, 1980). There were sales, too, of his sculptured bust, and even a hint that he took out shares in the railway he had denounced as 'the loathsomest form of devilry now extant' (Heeley, 1989). In his daily life, Wordsworth was disturbed and otherwise inconvenienced by the visitor influx to the Lake District, yet at the same time he was flattered that visitors sought him out, wishing to catch a glimpse of the great man he had become. The predictable postscript was that the poet's homes at Dove Cottage and Rydal Mount and his grave at Grasmere have become tourist shrines; the latter within close proximity to the Wordsworth Hotel and Spa. A further postscript is that so much of the 'development' that Wordsworth despised (the railway, the hotels, the steamboats plying the lakes, etc.) is now 'heritage' and the focus of contemporary conservation work.

While Wordsworth may have lost the battle in respect of the railway line, he can be seen as having won the war in the sense that he laid the foundation for a local conservation movement whose efforts helped spawn the National Trust in 1893. In 1951 the Lake District became a national park, endorsing his view that the Lakes were 'a sort of national property'. The attitudes Wordsworth embodied condition the extent and manner in which heritage is exploited for tourism purposes, and are reflected in the work of planning authorities, official environmental agencies, and the voluntary amenity lobby and in a host of other urban as well as rural conservation designations. The end-product is regulatory frameworks which nowadays control the nature and pace of tourism development, so that projects and proposals are only approved where they are judged to have minimal adverse impact on the host economy, society and environment. Tourism, therefore, exists somewhat uneasily alongside the green and sustainability agendas which are of such critical importance today. A further reason for writing the book was therefore to put this 'on the record', particularly the sense in which to date the tourist industry (and in that I include city tourism organisation) has so far paid only lip service to these vital agendas, a matter to which I return in the conclusion to this book.

Fourthly, another motive for putting pen to paper is the gap between the 'theory' of city marketing as evidenced in the academic literature and its 'practice'. Standard texts – from Kotler's *Marketing Places* (1993) to Morgan's *Destination Branding* (2004) and latterly Maitland and Ritchie's *City Tourism* (2009) – do not resonate with my 19 years of industry experience. This is even the case with texts written by former practitioners (notably Pike, 2004, 2008). So the third and perhaps heroic intent behind this book, is to try and blend academic theory with industry practice – to 'tell it like it is' as the 'sixties mantra went. A corollary of this is that the book is not written in the form of a conventional academic text with copious references and an ostensibly balanced and comprehensive assessment of the existing literature. Much of the raw material for this book is experiential and ultimately subjective, drawn from 'on the job' experience; directly as I plied my profession in Sheffield, Coventry, Birmingham and Nottingham, and indirectly as I shared experience with peers, particularly through the medium of European Cities Marketing (ECM). The latter is a network of European city tourist offices and convention bureaux who meet on a regular basis to exchange information and benchmark themselves in a spirit of trust, openness and camaraderie. Having said all of this, where relevant I have referred to key texts, articles, reports and presentations, and only Chapter 5 on setting up and leading city marketing agencies is overtly autobiographical. The remaining chapters are written in a more or less conventional academic style. Moreover, throughout the book I have set out conceptual frameworks within which it is possible to understand and otherwise make sense of city tourism and city tourism organisation. For these reasons, I believe the book has both empirical and theoretical value as an academic text.

Fifthly, I felt it was important in writing this book to provide a portrait of that very special breed of urban organisation which over a 19-year period provided me with a profession, livelihood, and so much travel, enjoyment and satisfaction! As we shall see in the next chapter, for the past 150 years urban authorities in Europe have responded to the growth of city tourism by setting up specialised marketing agencies. I will henceforth in this book refer generically to these bodies as either city tourism organisations (CTOs) or city marketing organisations (CMOs) – see the typology set out at the beginning of Chapter 1. As such, CTOs and CMOs are local-level destination marketing organisations (DMOs as these bodies are commonly referred to in the tourism business). CTOs and CMOs are to all intents and purposes the local scale counterparts of national tourist organisations (NTOs) such as Atout France, Czech Tourism, VVV Nederland, the Finnish Tourist Board and Visit Britain, and of regional tourist organisations (RTOs), for example Welcome to Yorkshire (formerly known as the Yorkshire Tourist Board), the Pori Regional Tourist Agency and Fjord Norway – the RTO for western Norway.

The rationale underpinning the existence of CMOs and CTOs everywhere – and for that matter NTOs and RTOs – is to lead and coordinate programmes of activity designed to raise destination profile, create more tourists (especially those staying overnight), and to then service visitor needs (especially for information) in order to increase length of stay and generate repeat custom. All of this activity is undertaken with a view to maximising the local economic gains associated with more visitors and enhanced city profile. However, despite having become nowadays more or less ubiquitous in cities, relatively little is 'known' about CTOs and CMOs in both popular and academic senses. Indeed, there is much confusion and ignorance surrounding their purpose and modus operandi, which is often controversial – no more so than when it embraces the branding of cities, as we shall subsequently see in Chapters 7 and 8. So the fifth motivation underpinning the writing of the book is to remedy this particular deficiency in the academic literature and in popular understanding, and to hopefully spread a little light on this much misunderstood and frequently undervalued and underloved form of urban organisation.

A sixth and final reason for writing the book is to deliver a European perspective. In 2002, I visited Turin to attend my first ever meeting of European Cities Marketing. I subsequently served on the ECM Board and became its Treasurer, and latterly I have acted in a private capacity as its

Internal Management Advisor. As I write, ECM has just appointed me to the position of Interim Chief Executive. Though I have done all of this good work, it remains the case that I have drawn far more from ECM than I have put back in, and one manifestation is this book's European perspective. In a nutshell, ECM acquainted me with how city tourism organisation is structured and managed outside of the United Kingdom.

The European perspective underpinning this book is important for two main reasons. First, it avoids parochialism and the blinkered and thoroughly complacent belief that we in the United Kingdom are somehow or other 'better' at city marketing than our mainland counterparts in the rest of Europe. On the contrary, we have much to learn from them, and as conveyed in this text the 'best practice' in city tourism organisation arguably lies less in the United Kingdom and more in Ireland, Scandinavia, Holland, Germany, Switzerland, Austria and Spain. Secondly, a European overview brings home the sense in which the similarities and continuities across national boundaries dwarf the differences and the discontinuities. The enduring needs which give rise to city tourism and city tourism organisation cross geographical boundaries, and the form and content of the organisational response to those self-same needs is much the same throughout Europe. Even the jargon and the proliferation of acronyms which characterise city marketing are shared; a 'bednight' in Iceland is literally a 'bednight' in Croatia; and MICE (meetings, incentives, conferences and exhibitions) in Luxembourg is MICE in Copenhagen!

With all their imperfections, the nine chapters that follow reflect and hopefully do some justice to all six of these motivations. As ever for the reader, the proof of the pudding will be in the eating!

Part 1
City Tourism

Chapter 1
Organising City Tourism

Introduction

It is a truism that tourism is a complex activity. At one and the same time, it may refer to a system of transport, an interaction of visitors and residents, a collection of trades and industries and to impacts of a commercial, eco-nomic, social and environmental kind. Unsurprisingly, therefore, 'tourism represents a serious challenge to man's ability to organise himself' (Young, 1973: 180). Further exploration of the organisational aspects of tourism are found in several sources (e.g. Elliott, 1997) and in a practical vein, they are neatly summarised in a remark made over 40 years ago by the then executive head of the British Travel Association (a forerunner of today's Visit Britain), whose name was Len Lickorish: 'there are, if anything, far too many cooks involved in tourism and I would like to say that there always will be and so our biggest problem is how to resolve the old difficulty that when you have too many interests and too many helpers, each one of whom can contribute a little, how do you get them all to work together' (cited in Heeley, 1975: 265). This chapter examines how in a city context tourism is typically organised so as to accommodate the multifaceted nature of the tourist industry with its private and public components and to deal with the attendant coordination issues. It begins by adumbrating a typology of city tourism organisation, before tracing its historical evolution. The final part of this chapter outlines the scope and content of the remainder of the book, providing *inter alia* a rationale for the case materials being utilised.

A Typology of City Tourist Organisations (CTOs) and City Marketing Organisations (CMOs)

This section presents an initial classification and clarification of the dif-ferent ways in which cities have sought in organisational terms to exploit the opportunities occasioned by tourism and to brand and otherwise 'posi-tion' themselves with respect to their image and reputation. In the absence of centralised national approaches, the scope and content of city tourism organisation has been shaped essentially by local needs and circumstances, but with much copying of precedent and best practice. Two main structural approaches have arisen; one is set within the city government and involves the establishment of a team of tourism officers grouped into a department (or section of a department) and reporting directly to local politicians; the second is the public–private partnership in which a more or less independent tourism agency is formed out of a coalition of stakeholders drawn from the local public and private sectors. Looking at individual nations and across Europe as a whole, the resultant mosaic or 'patchwork quilt' of the city government and public–private partnership-based initiatives appears at first sight to be confusing, almost to the point of being anarchic. As well as the local government versus public–private partnership dichotomy referred to above, from one city tourist organisation (CTO)/city marketing organisation (CMO) to the next there are considerable variations with respect to nomenclature, budget, extent of geographical coverage and operational responsibilities. Some CTOs/CMOs are narrowly focused with a limited range of accountabilities, while others are expansive, multifunctional marketing and communication exercises.

Figure 1.1 seeks to make sense of the heterogeneous nature of city tourism organisation, presenting a typology of CTOs and CMOs. City tourist organisations differ according to the degree to which they are responsible

City tourist organisations (CTOs)			
City leisure tourism bureau (CLTB) e.g. Ghent Tourism Department, Florence Tourist Board	**City convention bureau (CCB)** e.g. Congress Ghent, Florence Convention Bureau	**City tourist board (CTB)** e.g. Amsterdam Tourism and Convention Board, Zurich Tourism	
City marketing organisations (CMOs)			
City branding authority (CBA) e.g. Amsterdam Partners, Copenhagen Brand Secretariat	**City inward investment and business agency (CIIBA)** e.g. Amsterdam In Business, Invest in Nottingham	**City marketing agency (CMA)** e.g. Glasgow Marketing Bureau, Gothenburg & Co.	**City marketing and investment agency (CMIA)** e.g. Marketing Birmingham, Explore Northamptonshire

Figure 1.1 Typology of city tourism organisation

for attracting and servicing both leisure and business forms of tourism. City leisure tourism bureaux (CLTBs) are concerned only with leisure tourism, notably in the form of short-break holidaymakers and event-based tourists, while city convention bureaux (CCBs) address the so-called MICE sector – namely meetings, incentives, conventions and exhibitions. So for the Belgian city of Ghent, for instance, the Ghent Tourism Department (part of the city council) is the CLTB, while Congress Ghent (a public–private partnership) is the CCB. In many cities, however, leisure and business tourism functions are combined in the same organisation. This is the case, for instance, with the Munich Tourist Office and Visit Malmo (both part of the city government) and Zurich Tourism and the Amsterdam Tourism and Convention Board (ATCB) (both public–private partnerships). In Figure 1.1, I refer to these CTOs as city tourist boards (CTBs).

City marketing organisations (CMOs) are distinguishable from CTOs in that they are charged either with promoting city image generally (primarily through the vehicle of an overarching city brand) and/or with inward investment and business development functions. For instance, we shall see in Chapter 8 that Amsterdam Partners acts as the city branding authority (CBA), while Amsterdam in Business is the city inward investment and business agency (CIIBA). Both organisations exist independently of the CTB – the ATCB. A trend discernible in recent years is to combine tourism and city marketing functions into one organisation, and I refer in the typology to this type of body as a CMA – a city marketing agency. Brussels International and the Glasgow Marketing Bureau are examples. In the Scottish capital, Marketing Edinburgh will be established as a CMA next year, consolidating in one organisation the responsibilities of business and leisure tourism, film location marketing and city branding currently discharged by three separate organisations, namely the Destination Edinburgh Marketing Alliance, the Edinburgh Convention Bureau and the Edinburgh Film Focus. Finally, there are examples of a fourth kind of CMO – the city marketing and investment agency (CMIA) – in which tourism, city image/brand and inward investment/business development functions are delivered from within just one organisation. In England, for example, Marketing Birmingham has latterly become a case in point, as has the East Midlands city of Northampton through an agency known as Explore Northamptonshire.

In relation to the rest of the book, our organisational focus will be CTOs – all three kinds – as well as what we have referred to above as the CMA/CMIA forms of CMO. In Chapters 7 and 8 we will also consider the new breed of CBA which has recently emerged in Europe, especially in Germany and Holland. The typology presented in Figure 1.1 is, I believe, a useful starting point for a reader trying to come to grips with the otherwise arcane and sometimes perplexing organisational landscape represented by city tourism organisation. Another aid to understanding comes from tracing the historical origins and development of CMOs and CMAs, and it is this that we now discuss.

Evolution of City Tourism Organisation

Since time immemorial, there have been visitors to cities; the tourists have arrived and in their various ways been fulfilled, and for the city, there has been the resultant impact on economy, customs and landscape (de Botton, 2003). It can be argued that certain European cities such as Paris and London have been tourist destinations since as far back as Roman times. For sure, in the pre-industrial era the Grand Tour served as a finishing school for the British upper classes, connecting them with 'cultural' cities in Europe, amongst which were Paris, Rome, Turin, Basel, Berlin, Munich and Vienna (Black, 2003). Industrialisation and urbanisation in the 19th century to an extent shifted the focus of tourist movement from urban to rural, inducing a seasonal migration of humanity from town and city to sea and countryside. This movement of people came to symbolise leisure in the 19th and 20th centuries, and for Britain the classic account remains that of Pimlott (1947), as updated in several more recent books (e.g. Elborough, 2010; Walton, 1983).

While cities always remained significant for cultural and business tourism, it was not until the late 20th century that the focus of tourist movement began to shift once more in favour of the cities, reflected in a rapid expansion of convention, events and city break markets, both domestically and internationally. Key drivers of change were rising consumer affluence, low transport costs epitomised by carriers such as Ryanair and urban regeneration and reconstruction schemes. The latter not only boosted the touristic appeal of the long established 'great' cultural cities of Europe (Rome, Paris, Florence, Dubrovnik, Prague, Stockholm, Oslo, etc.), but also served to 'reinvent' industrial and/or war-damaged cities such as Glasgow, Warsaw, Rotterdam, Lodz, Birmingham, Barcelona, Genova and Dresden, emphasising their attractiveness as centres for business, culture, events, entertainment and shopping. A profound consequence of all of this, as we shall see amply demonstrated in the next chapter, is that the 'great indoors' of European cities are nowadays as sought after as the 'great outdoors' of coast and countryside.

The late 20th century also witnessed an upsurge of interest in city image and the related application of branding principles. To the best of my knowledge, this began in Europe in 1983 with the 'Amsterdam has it' and 'Glasgow's miles better' campaigns, both cities endeavouring to emulate the success of the 'I love New York' logo and slogan which had been introduced during the previous decade. In North America itself, the first CTO developments came just over 100 years ago (Weber & Chon, 2002), and they provide a useful point of contrast and comparison with the situation that was to emerge in Europe. In the United States and Canada, CTO organisations were to label themselves visitor and convention bureaux (VCBs). Reputedly, the first was established for Detroit in 1896. Many more were to follow in the next two decades, including the San Francisco Convention and Visitors Bureau whose formation in 1909 was triggered by the earthquake and fire that had famously devastated the city three years earlier. Most North American VCBs were (and are to this day) private organisations, with the greater part of their funding coming from hypothecated local bed taxes levied on commercial accommodation providers. Unsurprisingly, therefore, the raison d'être of VCBs is the generation of additional overnight stay business for those self-same accommodation providers – to put 'heads in beds' as the saying goes in the industry. At a national level, the interests of North American VCBs have been protected and networked for well over a century by an influential trade association – the International Association of Convention and Visitor Bureaux (from 2005 renaming itself *Destination Marketing Association International*).

In comparison, the first European CTOs came into existence more sporadically than was the case in North America, and they were from the beginning a much less uniform product shaped by essentially local circumstance and need. Though the evidence base is sketchy and incomplete, it appears that in Europe, Switzerland led the way in creating CTOs/CMOs. Certainly, the origins of what is now the *Lausanne Tourism and Convention Bureau* stretch as far back as 1866, and it may be regarded as Europe's oldest surviving urban destination marketing organisation. During the last two decades of the 19th century, a clutch of Swiss CTOs arose covering Geneva (1885), Zurich (1885), Basel (1890) and Lucerne (1892). Similar developments occurred in other European countries. Sweden's oldest city-based tourist organisation – the *Gotland Tourist Association* – was formed in 1896, bringing together tourism businesses and the municipality of Visby. A year later in Denmark, Copenhagen thought fit to establish a tourist promotional agency. In Holland, the antecedent of the ATCB is to be found in VVV Amsterdam; set up in 1902 to provide visitor information services in the Dutch capital. Over 100 years later, Amsterdam would be receiving nearly 5 million overnight stay tourists a year (see Chapter 2) and ATCB's 2008 income would be €8.9 million, derived more or less equally between local authority grants (52%) and private sector contributions/trading (48%).

As collaborations of the municipal authority and the city's tourism traders, these pioneering European CTOs foreshadowed what we have previously referred to as the public–private partnership, distinguishing them from their North American counterparts. In Europe, the prowess of public–private partnership as an organisational principle lay in a collective pooling of energies and monies across the public and private sectors which over time would lessen the burden on the local public purse – proportionately and, in some cases, absolutely. So, for instance, after a nearly 120-year history, *Basel Tourism* could in 2008 boast a multiplicity of local business partners, as well as an annual income of €7.4 million, of which only one-quarter derived from the local public sector. The remainder of the finances came from commercial membership fees (6%) and private sector contributions/trading income (69%). Similarly, the 2009 income of *Lucerne Tourism* amounted to €6.8 million, of which less than half (45%) derived from the public purse. Elsewhere in Switzerland, revenues from taxes on accommodation and other providers of tourist services have enabled the 125-year-old *Geneva Tourism and Convention Bureau* to be funded entirely from private sector and earned income sources. The Bureau's budgeted income for 2010 is €9.2 million, over two-thirds of which (67%) is from tourist taxes levied on the local tourist industry and the remainder from earned income. In Europe, however, CTOs and CMAs funded entirely from private sources remain the exception rather than the rule. Moreover, even when this does happen, as is the case with the Geneva Bureau, close working relationships with the local public sector are still evident. Indeed, this Bureau describes itself tellingly as a 'privately run public service association'. In addition to its mainstream conferencing, leisure tourism and visitor servicing operations, the Bureau through its events department is responsible for the city's annual street party and musical extravaganza each summer (the Geneva Festival). For the record, Geneva registered 2.9 million tourist bednights in 2008, with annual accommodation occupancy standing at 66.2%.

Throughout the 19th century and for the greater part of the 20th century, CTOs and CMAs (as was the case with national- and regional-level destination marketing organisations) adopted marketing practices invented and pioneered for travel agencies and tour operators by Thomas Cook in 1841 (Delgado, 1977). In that year, Cook and his brother John organised the world's first package tour, acting as an intermediary and connecting market to destination and venue through the medium of print. Throughout the nineteenth and twentieth centuries, CTOs and CMAs were to act in just such a fashion as print-based intermediaries; conducting advertising campaigns, publishing brochures and measuring success by the number of coupon responses. The advent in the late 1990s of the 'electronic age' (foreseen and labelled as such by Marshall McLuhan back in the 1960s) was to occasion a paradigm shift within city tourism organisation. McLuhan had predicted the world would become a 'global village' in which 'the medium is the message' (McLuhan, 1964). Although his vision of the future was not to unfold until the tail end of the 20th century, when it did, it quickly transformed CTOs and CMAs from paper to web and internet-based intermediaries, with huge consequences – strategic as well as operational.

Spurred on by a post-war 'boom' in tourism (Middleton & Lickorish, 2005) and the requirement felt by many cities to 'reinvent' themselves and cast off dated industrial and other reputations, more and more European cities had recourse to the establishment of CTOs and CMAs. As previously mentioned, this would in some instances involve setting up a tourism department or office of city government, staffed by council officers reporting to local politicians. Increasingly, however, initiatives of this kind led to some or other variant of a public–private partnership being employed. This organisational model sought to maximise commercial involvement and funding, though in practice such partnerships were afforded varying degrees of independence and managerial autonomy; from influenced by the local authority to a status which was truly independent and arms-length. During the post-war era the trend towards the public–private partnership mode of organisation was evident throughout nearly all parts of Europe, save for the countries of the old Eastern bloc – and even here, as we shall see, harbingers of public–private partnership were emerging. To an extent, increased application of public–private partnership aped the US-style VCB model – even in some cases using the terminology – but much more importantly it drew on the European precursors referred to previously, while at the same time reflecting economic liberalisation and the encouragement being given to local government to adopt 'new ways of working' with the private sector (Heeley, 2001: 279).

A fine example is Vienna where the signing of the State Treaty in 1955 meant that Austria regained its sovereignty, and in its capital one symbol of the withdrawal of the French, American, Russian and British occupying forces was the passing in that year of legislation permitting the formation of the *Vienna Tourist Board* (VTB). This organisation evolved into one of Europe's leading CTOs and it is illuminating briefly to outline its historical development. VTB began operation in February 1956 in offices boasting five telephone lines, 13 extensions, and a postal machine capable of handling 100 letters a day! As a collaboration between the local authority and the private sector, it was significant that the Board's staff were employed not by the municipality, but by the CTO direct '... reflecting the almost revolutionary ... separation of tourism from the administration of the city' (Vienna Tourist Board, 2006: 3). From the onset, VTB worked hand in glove with Austrian Air to promote a city destination with a rich cultural offer and an outstanding quality of life, capitalising on renowned architecture, music, palaces, museums, cafes and restaurants, and on icons as diverse as the Vienna Philharmonic Orchestra, the Danube, the Schonbrunn Palace, 'The Third Man', Breughel, Freud and shopping on Mariahilfer Strasse.

VTB's growth as a CTO mirrored the web and internet revolution to which we have previously referred, fuelling the expansion of Viennese tourism to the point where the city became a 'top ten' European city destination, attracting in 2008 some 10.2 million overnight stays worth €487 million to the core Vienna area. VTB's staffing complement increased from 32 in 1979 to 80 in 1991, while 4000 letters received from visitors in 1959 had by 2005 mushroomed to 125,000 inquiries by telephone, email, fax and mail. While in 1956 VTB had introduced a then state-of-the-art telephone-based hotel booking facility; it was able, by the end of the century, to offer intending visitors an online reservation service through the medium of its portal website. In 2008, this accommodation booking service handled 16,400 transactions, leading to 80,000 overnight stays. Roughly half of these came from web bookings, with the remainder generated by telephone and email. In the same year, VTB hosted more than 1000 media visits, working in partnership with the Austrian National Tourist Office and Austrian Air. A decade after the VTB had gone online at www.wien. info, this site was offering 4000 pages in 13 languages and receiving approximately 120,000 unique visitors a month.

VTB's high achieving convention department – the *Vienna Convention Bureau* – was established in 1969 in tandem with the privatisation of the Hofburg Congress Centre, and with financial support from the municipality and the chamber of commerce. The city's prowess as a location for conferences in the fields of medicine and the social and natural sciences was by 2008 worth an estimated €654 million to the city. Statistics published in 2008 by the International Congress and Convention Association ranked Vienna joint first with Paris as the world's leading international convention destination.

Vienna's 'almost revolutionary experimentation' with public–private partnership was followed by other cities in the country such as Linz, Salzburg and Innsbruck. In Austria's second city, for instance, the *Graz Tourist Office* was established in 1990 as a joint venture owned by the City of Graz (52%) and local commercial tourism interests (48%), reflecting the almost 'natural' requirement for public–private partnership in the case of organisations established to advance a particular branch of the economy.

In Germany, *Hamburg Tourism* was founded in 1989, and was the first CTO in that country to establish itself as a coalition of the relevant local authority and private sector interests. Its formation coincided with the political unification of the country, and other German cities soon followed the example of Hamburg in setting up CTOs as companies limited by guarantee. *Berlin Tourism Marketing* (BTM), for instance, was to begin life in 1993, gaining great impetus six years later from the opening of the reconstructed Reichstag. It nowadays has an annual budget in excess of €12 million; in 2009, the regional government – the Lander – provided 43% of its income, with the remainder drawn from a combination of trade contributions (12%) and earned income streams (45%). The principal shareholdings in the company are divided along the following lines: hotels (40%), banking (25%), the Lander (15%), airport (10%) and other tourism interests

(10%). Since its formation, BTM has presided over a period of sustained growth in convention and short-break traffic; the number of tourist bednights recorded in the city rose from 7.3 million in 1993 to stand at 18.9 million in 2009. Even in that year, as the economic recession occasioned downturns elsewhere in Europe – see Chapter 2 – Berlin's tourism recorded a year-on growth amounting to an estimated 1 million overnights, thanks largely to the 20th anniversary of the destruction of the Berlin Wall and the city's hosting of the 2009 World Championships in Athletics.

In France, as in Germany and Austria, public–private partnership also began to prevail in the post-war era, though the 'mixed economy' model employed there enabled the city governments to exert considerable influence and control. The *Paris Convention and Visitors Bureau* was set up as a not-for-profit public–private partnership in 1971, jointly owned by the city council and the local chamber of commerce and industry. France's second city set up a similar organisation in 1986 – *Lyon Tourism and Conventions*. An indicative and interesting example of a French CTO is *Avignon Tourism*; formed in 1974 with the public and private sector having 53% and 47% shareholdings, respectively. As well as mainstream marketing and visitor serving activities, Avignon Tourism manages the city's landmark bridge and palace. The CTO's 2009 income totalled €12.9 million, nearly all of it derived from trading revenues, with the palace and bridge between them making a contribution of over €9 million. The CEO of Avignon Tourism heads a staff of 179 (29% of whom are part time), reporting to a board of shareholders presided over by the mayor of the city.

In the Netherlands, a preoccupation with 'city marketing' – discussed in Chapter 8 – and a desire to fashion a more integrated delivery of urban destination marketing activities has led in the current decade to the formation of several CTOs/CBAs, mostly in the form of public–private 'foundations', amongst whom are Amsterdam Partners, Rotterdam Marketing, the Maastricht Region Branding Foundation, Dordrecht Marketing and Delft Marketing. *Delft Marketing*, for example, is a CTO established in 2004 as a foundation whose stakeholders are the municipality and the local tourist industry. It undertakes tourism promotions utilising a 'Delft creating history' slogan. Another CTO, *Rotterdam Marketing*, began life in 2001 as a result of merging the Rotterdam Convention Centre, VVV Rotterdam (the city tourist information service) and the Rotterdam Marketing Project Office which was a part of the City of Rotterdam Development Corporation.

In other European countries, city tourism administration remained more firmly wedded to the local authority. Belgium is a case in point: here the tourism authority for the cities of Antwerp, Bruges, Leuven and Ghent is a department (or a section of a department) of the city council. For example, Ghent City Council set up a tourism committee as far back as 1908, and became a member of Belgium's NTO – the Belgium Federation for the Promotion of Tourism. The *Ghent Tourism Department* followed in 1978, reflecting a desire on the part of Ghent City Council to pursue a more purposeful approach to the marketing of leisure tourism. The political 'boss' of the department is the Alderman for Culture, Tourism and Festivities. In contrast, the CMO for the Belgium capital is a public–private partnership. The origins of *Brussels International* lay in the hosting of Expo 58, and the associated requirement to provide visitor information services. The organisation was formally instituted as a tourist information service in 1960, and six years later took on additional tourism and city marketing functions. Designation as a 2000 European Capital of Culture provided a further stimulus to the development of the organisation. Nowadays, Brussels International draws approximately 45% of its income from earned and private sector sources, with the remainder coming from public bodies. It has five operating divisions for city marketing, events, visitor servicing, conventions and the Brussels Film Office, respectively. It is pioneering approaches to sustainable city marketing.

In Luxembourg City, capital of the Grand Duchy of Luxembourg – one of Europe's smallest sovereign states – a destination marketing organisation had been established as far back as December 1933. As a not-for-profit public–private collaboration, the *Luxembourg City Tourist Office* (LCTO) steadily expanded its operations during the post-war era; for instance, in 1953 just short of 10,000 enquiries were serviced by its municipal tourist information centre (TIC); by 1995, and with Luxembourg bearing the mantle of European City of Culture, the figure had risen to 288,000. Today, LCTO provides a comprehensive range of welcoming activities – from events to tour guides – and promotes externally across business and leisure tourism markets. For the year 2009, nearly three-quarters (74%) of its €4.9 million income comprised public sector grants from the national Ministry of Tourism and the city government. Although constituted as an independent public–private partnership and with just one city government representative on its governing board, the influence of the public sector is nonetheless significant, reflecting LCTO's financial gearing.

A flurry of CTO/CMA entities took root across the Iberian Peninsula during the last quarter of the 20th century. The *Madrid Tourist Board* dates from 1980 and is a marriage of the public and private sectors. This is reflected in its governance; a 15 strong board of trustees chaired by its President – a Madrid city councillor responsible for economy and employment. The remaining 14 'ordinary' members are drawn equally from the city government and the tourist trade. Operational activities of the Madrid Tourist Board are centred upon marketing the Spanish capital as a holiday and short-break destination, as well as visitor servicing through the management of tourist information services and guided tours and walks. The Madrid Convention Bureau (formed 1984) is now a department of *Madrid Promotions* – a city marketing company established by the Department of

Economy and Employment of Madrid City Council. Three autonomous public–private collaborations – the *Valencia Tourism and Convention Bureau* (VTCB), *Bilbao Tourism* and the *Gijon Joint Tourist Board* – were set up in 1991, 1992 and 1994, respectively.

The VTCB is an interesting example of how public–private partnership has been used to optimise the use of local government monies and the delivery of activities traditionally provided by the state. As Spain's third-largest city, Valencia underwent a remarkable expansion of its tourist sector during the last decade of the 20th century, with the number of over-night stays more than quadrupling between 1992 and 2007. In the latter year, Valencia emphasised its new found status as a tourist destination by hosting the America's Cup yachting race. Growth on such a scale was made possible by renovating the city's historic heritage, making accessible its adjacent beach area, and by developing a clutch of fine conference venues as well as a sensationally iconic complex – the City of the Arts and Science – complete with viewing point, opera house, interactive science museum and Europe's largest aquarium. VTCB was established to create awareness of these assets, and to work with carriers and the local tourism sector to grow business and leisure tourism traffic. Established as a not-for-profit private foundation, it has approximately 250 private sector members, with Iberian Airlines and Heineken currently acting as corporate sponsors. Its annual budget is approximately €8 million, three-quarters of which is provided by the city government with the remainder coming from membership fees and earned income streams. All VCTB staff are employed directly by the foundation, on terms and conditions comparable to those which obtain in the private sector. Similarly, *Barcelona Tourism* (1993) arose as a private foundation in the aftermath of the 1992 Olympic Games in order to capitalise on the city's enhanced profile and the legacy of sporting and other tourist infrastructure – see Chapter 3. In Portugal's capital city, and in anticipation of hosting Expo '98, *Lisbon Tourism* was set up as a non-profit organisation in 1997. A partnership of the municipality and tourism trader interests, Lisbon Tourism has since 2003 undertaken international destination marketing for the wider regional area under a delegation arrangement with the Portuguese national tourist office. It sees itself as a model of public–private partnership, with over 500 associate members drawn from the private sector.

An early example of Scandinavian CTO development was the *Helsinki Tourist and Convention Bureau* which was created in 1963 as a public–private partnership, though it remains wholly owned by the municipality. Elsewhere in Finland, *Espoo Convention and Marketing* (2001) is jointly owned by the municipality and local tourism businesses, as is *Turku Touring*. The latter organisation's city region approach embraces the historic port city of Turku situated in south west Finland on the shores of the Baltic, as well as no less than 27 adjoining municipalities spread across the surrounding archipelago. The City of Turku and eight private sector tourism operators are the company's equity shareholders. While the bedrock of financial support is provided by the City of Turku, this is supplemented by industry contributions from the eight operators referred to above; these include hotel and spa complexes, as well as meeting venues and visitor attractions such as the Moominworld children's theme park.

Other city regions in Finland have CTOs as a part of the local government administration, for example, Pori and Oulu. In the latter instance, destination marketing and visitor servicing activities are undertaken by a tourism team led by a senior officer (the Marketing Director) who reports to the head of the Innovation and Marketing Department of Oulu City Council. The annual municipal subsidy received by the tourism team is currently in the region of €1 million, with additional financial support from the private sector with respect to the principal holiday and convention marketing campaigns. In Scandinavia's most northerly country, Iceland, an approach based on the local authority is evident in the capital where *Visit Reykjavik* was established in 2003 as the tourism section of the Department of Culture and Tourism.

In Sweden, the origins of the *Stockholm Visitors Board* lay in an organisation formed in 1935 to attract tourists to the Swedish capital. The post-war years saw the opening in 1953 of a city centre TIC coinciding with the 'Stockholm Celebrates 700 Years' festivities. Stockholm City Council's visitor servicing activities were complemented in 1980 by the advertising and promotional work of Destination Stockholm. The latter body emerged as a joint initiative bringing together the City Council's Stockholm Information Service, the Stockholm County Council, and the Stockholm Hotels and Restaurants Association. Its pioneering holiday and city break promotions included the 'Stockholm Package' which linked to the 'Stockholm Card' with event and theatre ticketing. Destination Stockholm was wound up in 2001, and its activities and that of the Stockholm Information Service were subsequently absorbed by the Stockholm Visitors Board, an operating arm of the Stockholm Business Region Board wholly owned by Stockholm City Council. The Stockholm city card exemplifies the impact of technology, with the first version in 1982 being paper based. In 1995, these were replaced by magnetic cards, and in 2008, a digitalised, smart card version was introduced.

Elsewhere in Sweden, cooperation across the public and private sectors is evident in the formation of Uppsala Tourism (1988) and Visit Lulea (2004). By way of illustration, *Uppsala Tourism* is a limited company owned jointly by the municipality (51%), the county authority and local tourism trader interests. Its annual income is currently in the region of €1.9 million, split between local authority grants and private sector/earned income streams to the tune of 70% and 30%, respectively. In the spring of 2011, Uppsala Tourism will be restructured and its activities absorbed within a wider organisation administering all the city marketing functions currently discharged by the municipality. A similar sort of restructuring is planned with regard to *Visit Lulea*; this organisation was formed on the initiative of the local authority and there are currently 90 private sector members who together provide approximately one-third of the organisation's annual budget which is in the region of €800,000 – the remainder of the financial support derives from the municipality (50%) and other public sector agencies (20%). In Sweden's second city, *Gothenburg & Co* is likewise constituted as a public–private partnership and – as we shall see in Chapter 3 – has pursued a particularly effective approach to sourcing, attracting and hosting (and in some cases producing) major events. In contrast to the CTOs established for Uppsala, Lulea and Gothenburg, *Malmo Tourism* (1990) exists as a department of the local authority.

In Denmark, *Wonderful Copenhagen* was set up in 1992 as a non-profit foundation, though as we have seen its roots stretched back much further to 1897. Nowadays, it has 60% of its budget emanating from non-public sources. As with Gothenburg & Co, it is noteworthy for having strong major events capabilities. In Denmark, the cities of Aarhus, Odense and Aalborg have established independent public–private foundations through *Visit Aarhus*, *Visit Odense* and *Visit Aalborg*. Likewise in Norway, the *Bergen Tourist Board* was formed in 1982 as a joint municipal and private sector venture. It now has upwards of 400 commercial members and it is the major shareholder in Fjord Norway – the official destination marketing organisation for the Norwegian Fjords. *Visit Oslo* emerged in 1991 as a limited company jointly owned by the municipality and local tourist trader interests, replacing the former local authority department and promotional foundation. It was soon to be at the forefront of the new internet technologies, launching www.visitoslo.com early in 1996. The site currently attracts over 1 million unique visits a year.

As far as Britain is concerned, the first arms-length CTO was set up in Plymouth in 1978 (Heeley, 2001). The *Plymouth Marketing Bureau* was constituted as a company limited by guarantee, governed by a board of directors of whom six were nominated by the local authority and nine elected from the ranks of tourism trader interests. A decade later, nearly half of the annual expenditure was derived from non-local authority sources and cost effectiveness was being trumpeted (Heeley, 2001). Several more independent, arms-length CTOs/CMAs followed the example of Plymouth; amongst them are the *Birmingham Convention and Visitor Bureau* (1982), the *Greater Glasgow Tourist Board* (1983) and the *Merseyside Tourism and Conference Bureau* (1985). The catalyst for the establishment of the latter organisation and its core funder was an urban development agency – the Merseyside Development Corporation – appointed by the national government in the wake of the 1981 Toxteth Riots in Liverpool. In the second half of the 1980s, two more CTOs were established; *Leicester Promotions*

(1986) and *York Visitor and Conference Bureau* (1987). In the next decade, the Birmingham, Liverpool and Glasgow initiatives were used as role models for the creation of arms-length CTOs/CMOs, including *Edinburgh Convention Bureau* (1990), *Marketing Manchester* (1991), *Destination Sheffield* (1991), *Coventry and Warwickshire Promotions* (CWP) (1996) and the *Newcastle and Gateshead Initiative* (2000). Destination Sheffield, CWP (now called CVI) and the Newcastle Gateshead Initiative were notable as proto-types of fully integrated destination marketing communications exercises – what we have referred to in the typology as CMAs. Here, in addition to functions centred on tourism were the related fields of city imaging and event production and management. *Profile Nottingham*, launched at the end of the 1990s combined tourism and city imaging roles working along-side a separate convention bureau called *Conference Nottingham*.

The first decade of the 21st century was to see a further strengthening and consolidation of CTOs in England, presided over by a new national network of government-funded regional development agencies. For instance, destination marketing of the historic city of Chester has from 2004 been undertaken by the *Cheshire and Warrington Tourist Board* – a three-legged partnership of the North West Development Agency, the local authorities and the private sector. Most of the tourist boards set up under the aegis of regional development agencies have set a city or cities within a wider, mainly rural geographical area, for example Northampton and *Explore Northamptonshire* (2004), Sheffield and *Yorkshire South*, Leeds and Bradford and the *West Yorkshire Area Tourism Partnership* and Hull and the *Hull and East Yorkshire Tourism Partnership*. Elsewhere in the current decade, the York Visitor and Conference Bureau reorganised itself as *Visit York* (2008) (see the case study comprising Chapter 6) and in the following year, the Carlisle City Council privatised its tourism services via the for-mation of *Carlisle Tourism Partnership*. Profile Nottingham and Conference Nottingham were absorbed into Experience Nottingham (2003) which, in turn, relaunched itself one year later as *Experience Nottinghamshire*. Birmingham Convention and Visitor Bureau (BCVB) became part of *Marketing Birmingham* in 2002, and the GGTB was restructured as the *Glasgow Marketing Bureau* in 2005. The historical evolution of Market-ing Birmingham and Glasgow Marketing Bureau are documented in Chapter 3, while the setting up of Marketing Birmingham, Experience Nottinghamshire and CWP form part of Chapter 5. For the moment, suf-fice to say that the contemporary landscape of city tourism organisation in Britain is dominated by arms length public–private partnerships.

In Italy, city tourism organisation has historically centred on the munic-ipality. CTOs there typically present themselves as departments of the city administration, funded by the municipality and staffed by civil servants – for example the *Florence Tourist Board*, the *Milan Tourism Department* and the *Rome Tourism Office*. *Genoa Tourism* (2002) – also a department of the

municipality – can be seen as a response to the decline of that city's traditional steel, coke, shipbuilding and port industries, and the need in particular to capitalise on the city's 2004 designation as a European Capital of
Culture. However, there are signs in Italy of experimentation with public–
private organisational forms. For example, *Turin Tourism* was formed in
1997 as an amalgamation of three hitherto separate agencies, and is a not-
for-profit public–private sector venture. In Greece, the *Athens Tourism and
Economic Development Company* – with its 'breathtaking Athens' slogan –
has undertaken destination marketing activities for the capital since its
hosting of the Olympic Games in 2004. The Athens Convention Bureau
operates as a more or less independent section of the Company.

In Eastern Europe, the city tourism organisation is mostly discharged
through a department of the local authority. This is the case, for instance,
with Budapest and Tallinn. The *Budapest Tourism Office* (BTO) was created in 1996 by the city government of the Hungarian capital, bringing
under one roof the tourism marketing, event promotion and visitor servicing activities previously undertaken by a number of separate public
agencies. BTO has approximately 40 employees, led by its Director, all of
whom are employees of the municipality. The *Tallinn City Tourist Office* is
a section of the Department of City Enterprise. It was established in 2000
as the Estonian capital sought to take advantage of the upsurge in tourism which had followed the re-establishment of independence in 1991.
In that year, just 250,000 overnight visitors were recorded: by 2008, a
near fivefold expansion had occurred, and of the 1.2 million visitors 86%
were foreign with an average length of stay of 2.4 nights. The profile of
visiting tourists in Tallinn was a somewhat discordant 'market mix' of
'cultural' and 'hen and stag' motivations. This mix has come to characterise European city tourism – from Nottingham, Newcastle and Dublin,
through to Amsterdam, Prague, Cracow, Riga and Sofia. The Tallinn City
Tourist Office itself comprises 25 local government officials, of whom
nine work in the tourist information service. In Estonia's second city,
Tartu, tourism marketing functions for the city and its rural hinterland
are discharged by the *Tartu County Tourism Federation*. This organisation
was established in 1999 by the municipal authority and other local
authorities making up the county administration. Tartu Convention
Bureau is a section of the Federation. Currently, the Deputy Mayor of
Turku City Council responsible for government, administration and
business presides over the Federation.

Local government departments also characterise CTOs in the Polish
cities of Warsaw, Lodz and Wroclaw. The *Warsaw Tourist Office* (including
the Warsaw Convention Bureau) is a department of the City Council, with
its activities financed wholly from the city budget. In the Ukraine, the city
administration of Odessa has a Department of Tourism, while a team of
four tourism officers is part of the *Lviv Office of Culture and Tourism*.

The economic and social restructuring of Eastern Europe over the past two decades has, however, occasioned more commercially based approaches and joint venture arrangements. In Riga – the capital of Latvia – a new tourism development bureau on has just been launched. A further example is Prague, whose tourism industry grew rapidly after 1989 and the so-called Velvet Revolution. The bulk of its 73,000 bedspaces have been built since then, and the capital of the Czech Republic now absorbs annually in the region of 12 million overnight stays, compared to 2 million in 1989. Interestingly, this sixfold expansion in volume has occurred with little or no national- or city-level investment in marketing, though significant visitor servicing activities are in evidence as Prague seeks to make the most of burgeoning tourist numbers. Although the origins of the *Prague Information Service* stretch back to 1958, as an organisation it underwent radical post-1989 change and expansion in response to the capital's mushrooming popularity. It now runs four TICs, and since 1995 has managed the city's official tourist web portal (Novotny, 2007). As well as information, ticketing and accommodation booking, the Service offers guided walks and tours and is responsible for the Prague visitor card. Interestingly, it also markets and manages several historic monuments in the city. Entrance charges and souvenir sales from these monuments form a significant income stream which effectively cross-subsidises the other 'loss-making' information service activities provided annually at a net cost of approximately €500,000 a year.

Promoting the conference tourism offer in the Czech capital is a not-for profit association, the *Prague Convention Bureau*. Set up in 2008 along decidedly Western European lines, it established in its first year a convention bureau infrastructure comprising: conference guide, website, ambassador, and online bidding capabilities. For 2009, two thirds of its €310,000 income derived from private sector sources, including substantial sponsorship from the brewing giant Pilsner Urquell.

On a pan-European level, the European Federation of Conference Towns was established in 1964 to represent the interests of CCBs, and European Cities Tourism followed in 1988 to network city tourist offices in order to promote best practice and information sharing. Both organisations amalgamated in 2007 to become *European Cities Marketing* (ECM), arguably symbolising a 'coming of age' of city tourism organisation in Europe.

Format of the Remainder of the Book

The rest of the book comprises eight chapters. The one which follows – *Measuring City Tourism* – examines the demand for urban tourism in Western Europe from the vantage point of how typically (and imperfectly!) we measure its volume, value and impact, as well as the marketing activity with which it is associated. While the broad commercial and economic significance of city tourism can be established accurately and comprehensively, intercity benchmarking and the evaluation of marketing performance remain for the most part, work in progress. Chapter 3 – *The Dynamics of City Tourism* – elaborates upon the respective roles of the private and public sectors in city tourism, as a prelude to 'mini' case studies that chart the post-war tourist development of five European cities, comparing and contrasting how each has been successful in repositioning themselves in image terms and in growing their local tourism industries from a low base. Dublin, Glasgow, Gothenburg, Barcelona and Birmingham have been chosen carefully as case studies to represent northern, western and southern European contexts, and on the basis of three other considerations: firstly, the five cities and the city tourism organisation each has established are widely recognised in the industry as role models; secondly, in each instance, tourism has been used as a basis to create in seemingly unpropitious circumstances a new, post-industrial identity; and thirdly, the five cases permit market- and supply-based approaches to growing city tourism to be compared and contrasted.

Part 2 of the book goes on to set out an explanatory framework within which to conceptualise and appraise CTO/CMA activities. Chapter 4 – *City Tourism Organisation: Structure and Operations* – delineates the respective roles of governance and executive, and reviews programmes and principal activity areas, exemplifying the marketing, communications, and visitor servicing activities of CTOs/CMAs. The greater part of the case material in this chapter derives from a study of the structure and operations of the Vienna Tourist Board (VTB). The rationale for this lies partly in the exemplary fashion in which the Board prepares (and makes readily available) data and other information relating to its history, governance, departmental organisation and current activities. More important, however, is the Board's reputation for quality service delivery, alongside the sheer scale and demonstrable cost effectiveness of its operations. Chapter 5 – *Setting Up and Leading City Marketing Organisations* – identifies and exemplifies the 'building blocks' that need to be put in place when setting up CTOs/CMAs 'from scratch', namely funding, governance, professional staff, offices, IT infrastructure, brand platform and private sector engagement. It highlights the principal leadership challenges by reference to 'key lessons learned', drawing on the author's experience over a 19-year period at Sheffield, Coventry, Birmingham and Nottingham. By its very nature, the case material here is self-selecting; the experience referred to above was readily 'on tap', whereas published sources of information bearing on the establishment and leadership of CMOs were to all intents and purposes non-existent.

The conceptual framework established in Chapters 4 and 5 are then exemplified in Chapter 6 titled *City Tourism Organisation Case Study: York, United Kingdom*. This chapter examines the impact of tourism in the city and its post-war development as a backdrop to considering the evolution and contemporary activities of the CTO, namely Visit York. The choice of York is premised on the city's European status as a tourism destination, as well as the success of the CTO in maximising private sector and earned income streams, in attempting to reconcile its city marketing activities with conservation interests and the needs of local residents, and in securing awards as prestigious as that of *'European Tourism City of the Year'*.

Part 3 considers city branding, and how CMAs and CBAs are implementing these topical and inherently controversial projects. Chapter 7 – *The Problematic Nature of City Branding* – reviews the scope and content of such campaigns by referring to 20 European cities. It does so within a framework of a seven-part structure and a five-stage process, taking into account the limitations of city branding as well as its great potential. This is followed by Chapter 8 – *City Branding in the Netherlands* – in which city branding and CBAs are examined with particular reference to campaigns in The Hague and Amsterdam. The former illustrates the pitfalls of city branding, while the latter warrants in-depth appraisal because it is fast emerging as a role model for cities elsewhere in Holland and Europe.

Part 4 draws together the various strands and assesses the future prospects of city tourism and city tourism organisation. Chapter 9 – *Whither City Tourism and City Tourism Organisation?* – reviews progress made to date and examines the future prospects of city tourism as a market force whose rapid year on growth since the 1990s was abruptly halted by the 2007–2009 global recession. It suggests that a watershed has been reached in 2010, both for city tourism and city tourism organisation, highlighting the key challenges which lie ahead against a backdrop of financial sustainability, social media and other considerations.

Chapter 2
Measuring City Tourism

Introduction

Tourism refers to transitory movements of people who leave their home environments for business and leisure purposes: the tourists, as such, may go for a day or stay overnight (Heeley, 1980a). The sheer magnitude of tourism to and within Europe is nowadays such as to defy easy portrayal and comprehension. According to the European Travel Commission, spending by international and domestic tourists in 2008 amounted to €32 billion, resulting in 20 million jobs, and accounting for 5% directly (and 10% indirectly) of European gross domestic product. An estimated 2 million firms are active in the tourism sector, and Europe's share of international tourist arrivals is a dominating 53%.

On a pan-European basis and at an individual country level, it is frustratingly difficult to estimate in precise terms the amounts of domestic and international tourism attributable to cities as destinations. Partly this reflects the 'broad brush' national basis on which so much tourism data are collected, collated and published which does not permit accurate city-level disaggregation. It also reflects a multilayered set of definitional issues. Cities and their tourism do not fit easily into conventional distinctions between different forms of tourism destination – heritage/cultural, seaside/coastal, countryside/rural and town/urban. Bath, for instance, is heritage/cultural, but it is also a city, just as Nice is seaside/coastal, but also a city. Having said all this, the evidence we have, drawn from national-level surveys, indicates that cities in early 21st century Europe are the primary tourist destinations for both international and domestic visitors. Statistics prepared and presented at a city-level provide further compelling indications of how powerful a magnet urban destinations are, especially for the so-called 'discretionary' business and leisure tourist staying overnight – the conference, exhibition and congress delegate, the holidaymaker and the visitor 'taking in' some or other aspects of a city on a short break. Discretionary overnight stay traffic, it should be emphasised, is the all-important 'battlefield' on which destination marketing organisations, urban and rural, compete for business. Non-discretionary forms of overnight stay tourism – a trip necessitated by business or by the need or desire to see a friend and relative (the so-called visits to friends and relatives (VFR) traffic) – are by definition more or less uninfluenced by marketing activity. The day visitor – relatively low in spending and high on mainte-nance – is 'managed' rather than promoted, as exemplified in the York case study in Chapter 6.

To state the obvious, tourists visiting cities make up city tourism, and as with all forms of tourism – be they urban or rural in geographical inci-dence – there are attendant impacts on the host destination and commu-nity. Again, fairly self-evidently, there is a requirement to measure and otherwise scope out both the nature and extent of the tourist influx and the impacts to which it gives rise. City tourism is therefore measured in terms of its *volume, value* and *socio-demographic characteristics* and its *costs* and *benefits*, and there is a wide variety of measurement methods and techniques: some of these are quantitative and others qualitative; and while some of them may be regarded as rigorous and scientific, others are decidedly more subjective and judgemental. The conventional classifica-

	Costs	Benefits
Economic	e.g. public authority costs	e.g. income and employment
Social	e.g. crowding, congestion, corrupted culture and values, and resident antagonism	e.g. enhanced leisure and cultural opportunities
Environmental	e.g. loss of amenity, pollution, wear and tear on historic buildings	e.g. "cash incentive to conserve" supplied by tourism

Figure 2.1 The economic, social and environmental costs and benefits of city tourism

tion of impacts gives us six boxes corresponding to the economic, social and environmental costs and benefits of tourism (see Figure 2.1). In each box at a city level, there is usually measurement activity of some or other sort going on. Assessing economic costs gauges amongst other things the effects of city tourism on the public purse – the public sector investment in marketing and supporting infrastructure and superstructure, ranging from roads, leisure and cultural facilities, through to convention centre subsidy, toilets, refuse collection and police. Set against these costs are economic benefits, and of great significance here is the expenditure, income and employment associated with tourism. For instance, tourism in the English city of York accounted in 2007 for 4.1 million visitors who spent €415 million, generating in the region of 10,646 full-time equivalent (FTE) jobs.

The aim of this chapter is to give the reader a flavour of the order of magnitude of city tourism in terms of volume, expenditure and economic benefits and an understanding of the ways in which these parameters are typically measured and presented by CTOs/CMAs themselves as well as by researchers in universities, government agencies and observatories. Having said that the volume, value and economic benefits of city tourism are the prime concerns of this chapter, it is important not to lose sight of the 'bigger picture' summarised in Figure 2.1. In every city there is an almost bewildering variety of costs and benefits engendered by tourism other than the economic gains. Beginning with Young (1973), as updated by Brown (1998), the arguments and evidence have been exhaustively set out in the literature, and the consensus may be summarised as follows. Though the economic costs are notoriously difficult to measure, it is important for city politicians and managers to bear these in mind. What evidence we have, however, indicates that the local economic benefits of tourism are appreciably outweighed by the public authority costs (Heeley, 1980b). As for the social costs, there is no doubting that congestion, overcrowding and erosion of indigenous culture and values is occasioned by tourism, and that it finds expression in some local residents feeling 'hard done by'. Such costs are palpable yet inherently subjective, varying from one individual to the next. The author first came across 'I'm not a tourist, I live here' badges in London in the early 1970s, but in this and other European cities anti-tourism sentiment is more of a whimper than a backlash. Resident opinion surveys also indicate that perceptions of social disbenefits are outweighed by those relating to the economic gains and to the very real social benefits consequent upon the enhanced amenities and environments which characterise urban tourist destinations. The same sort of argument applies to the different, but no less emotive and serious issues surrounding the environmental costs and benefits of city tourism. Sheer pressure of people and their accoutrements impairs and even destroys cityscapes and urban environments – as any visitor to London,

Venice, Prague, Paris, Rome, Oxford, Dubrovnik and Andorra La Vella can testify. Set against this are the environmental benefits that tourism engenders: for cities endeavouring to survive in a utilitarian world, tourism supplies an all-important 'cash incentive to conserve', as we demonstrate in the city case study of York in Chapter 6.

In brief, the author believes that it is useful to distinguish between (1) measurement activity useful for giving us guidance on how we can best manage tourism's economic costs and its deleterious social and environmental drawbacks and (2) the measurement activity used to assess the volume, value and economic benefits of city tourism, and the related performance of the urban tourist sector and its CTO/CMA. It is to the latter measures that we now turn our attention in the remainder of this chapter.

Types of Measurement

City tourism and the marketing activity with which it is associated are typically measured by four sets of measurement parameters. Each of these parameters requires an appropriate method and research vehicle to be put in place, so that city tourism organisation can appraise and evaluate its tourism sector and its CTO/CMA. As the management guru Peter Drucker famously remarked: 'If you can't measure it, you can't manage it'. Intuitively, this applies with great force to the world of city tourism, though there is in practice less than perfect adherence to Drucker's dictum. Research is often the 'cinderella' of CTO/CMA operations; a technical, somewhat esoteric 'optional extra' which can be afforded a low priority (or even dispensed with altogether) in favour of operating exigencies. Notwithstanding this, the four measurement parameters in city tourism are as follows.

First, it is important to measure and monitor the volume of city tourism in terms of trips, bednights and occupancy – I refer to these as the critical *industry measures*. Secondly, there are the equally important *community measures*. With reference to the city economy, community measures demonstrate the value of tourist expenditure, and the resultant local income and employment generated by that expenditure through the so-called multiplier process. Thirdly, evaluation research is undertaken to calculate the economic returns from the marketing campaigns undertaken by CTOs/CMAs which are designed to generate more business or leisure tourists. These are the *marketing measures* which enable the efficiency of CTO/CMO marketing activities to be rigorously evaluated. Marketing measures represent a separate strand of monitoring and intelligence to the industry and community measures to which previous reference has been made. To repeat, all three measurement parameters need to be in place in order to undertake objective assessment of the performance of the city's tourist industry and its city tourism organisation. Great added value accrues from doing this over time and against a base bar. Further value is forthcoming when performance can be appraised against that of other comparable cities – nationally and internationally. In this way, *intercity benchmarking* can be seen to form the fourth and final category of measurement parameter. Unfortunately, as we shall see later, it is at present undertaken only fitfully and incompletely. We shall now consider in turn each of the four measurement parameters.

Measurement of Volume: Industry Measures

The three measures of volume routinely encountered in city tourism and much reported on are tourist trips, bednights and hotel occupancy. In terms of *tourist trips*, there is typically a disaggregation into international/ domestic categories and into those tourists staying overnight and those visiting for the day. On that basis, for instance, we can reliably say that nowadays cities account for roughly 40% of all international tourist arrivals. Each year Euromonitor publishes a league table of the so-called 'top' 150 tourist cities in the world as measured by the number of international overnight trips (Table 2.1). The reader can see that for the year 2008 this put London in poll position with 15 million trips/arrivals. The next four European cities to appear in the table were Paris, Rome, Barcelona and Dublin, occupying 6th, 14th, 18th and 19th position, respectively.

Table 2.2 utilises the data collated by ECM relating to 2006, the last year of the city tourism 'boom' which characterised the late 20th and early 21st centuries (Ponti & Sager, 2009). It shows Europe's 10 most-visited city tourist destinations in that year, as measured by the combined number of domestic and international overnight trips. The volume of tourism to London panned out at a massive 26.6 million trips, as befits Europe's largest city and erstwhile tourist destination. Paris was next registering 16.3 million trips, while the remaining eight cities shown in Table 2.2 recorded impressive volumes within a 4.4 million–11.1 million range. When these data are examined over time, as in the comparison with 2000 contained in

Table 2.1 Tourist arrivals at selected European cities 2008

Ranking	*(millions)*
1 London	15.0
6 Paris	8.4
14 Rome	6.2
18 Barcelona	4.9
19 Dublin	4.5

Source: Euromonitor (2010)

Table 2.2 Tourist trips to Europe's top 10 tourist cities 2006

		Overnight tourist trips* (millions)	*Percentage ± since 2000*
1	London	26.6	−16
2	Paris	16.3	+11
3	Rome	11.1	+77
4	Madrid	8.6	+50
5	Barcelona	7.2	+99
6	Berlin	7.1	+41
7	Dublin	5.7	+33
8	Amsterdam	4.7	+16
9	Vienna	4.4	+24
10	Munich	4.4	+17

*Tourists – domestic and international staying visitors using commercial accommodation forms, excluding VFR
Source: ECM/TourMis (2007)

Table 2.2, they indicate the extraordinary growth rates then being enjoyed by these cities. Barcelona and Rome, for instance, experienced 99% and 77% growth, respectively, in the volume of overnight stay tourism between 2000 and 2006, while the comparable figures for Madrid, Berlin and Dublin were 50%, 41% and 33%, respectively. The late 20th/early 21st century vogue for city-based short breaks and conventions, fuelled as it was by low-cost air travel, is wonderfully captured in these statistics whose original sources are national-level exit and household surveys conducted by public authorities. The relevant data for the London figures in Table 2.2, for instance, are derived from the annual United Kingdom Tourism Survey and the International Passenger Survey.

Tourist bednights and related *accommodation occupancy* data are also important indicators of tourist volume, enabling profiles and performance of the city tourism sector to be chartered more insightfully and analytically. Bednights are in many respects the truest indicator of tourist volume in that such data allow variations in length of stay to be taken into account. If we compare Tables 2.2 and 2.3, for instance, we can see that while Amsterdam outdistances Munich in terms of the volume of trips, the opposite is the case in respect of tourist bednights because average length of stay in Munich is longer than in Amsterdam. Table 2.3, by disaggregating bednights into domestic and international categories, reveals how Vienna, Amsterdam, Budapest, Brussels and Dubrovnik share a

Table 2.3 Bednights generated in selected European cities 2007

	Bednights (millions)	*Percentage (domestic)*	*Percentage (international)*
Berlin	17.3	62	38
Barcelona	11.7	32	68
Vienna	10.4	18	82
Munich	9.5	57	43
Amsterdam	8.8	17	83
Budapest	6.1	15	85
Stockholm	5.6	59	41
Copenhagen	5.3	38	62
Brussels	5.1	14	86
Dubrovnik	1.8	10	90

Source: ECM/TourMis (2008)

proportionately heavy dependence on foreign visitors. In these cities, foreign tourists account for more that four out of every five bednights. In contrast, Berlin, Munich and Stockholm are reliant mainly on domestic market segments, to the tune of 62%, 57% and 59%, respectively. Intercity reporting of bednight statistics enables comparisons and contrasts to be

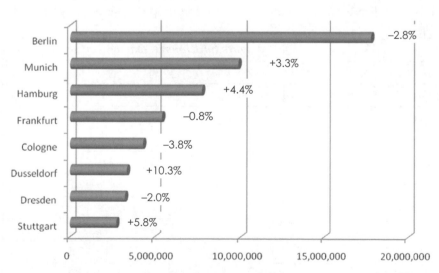

Figure 2.2 Comparison of selected German cities by tourist bednights in 2008: Number of bednights and percentage year-on growth or decline

drawn: for example, Figure 2.2 shows the bednight volumes recorded by leading German cities for the year 2008. As might be expected, Berlin is leading the way with over 17 million bednights, followed by Munich (9.8 million) and Hamburg (7.7 million). Frankfurt, Cologne, Dusseldorf, Dresden and Stuttgart lie within a 2.7–5.4 million bednight range. Interestingly, the largest year on growth rates were registered by Dusseldorf and Stuttgart with 10.3% and 5.8%, respectively, while Frankfurt, Cologne, Dresden and Berlin experienced year-on reductions, reflecting the global economic recession.

Because bednight statistics factor in length of stay variations, there is every reason to use them so as to indicate the pecking order of European city tourism. On this basis, Table 2.4 uses just released 2009 returns to show Europe's top 10 city tourism destinations, and the year-on reductions/increases experienced by each of them. London and Paris, recording massive 45 million and 34 million figures, respectively, are pre-eminent, with a combined volume nearly equal to that of the other eight cities. Reflecting the economic recession, seven cities experienced year-on downturns in volume between 2% and 8%.

Accommodation occupancy is monitored on a continuous basis in most cities and is a key barometer-type indicator of tourism demand. Occupancy levels in cities vary by week and by season. During the week, demand is typically more robust from Monday to Thursday, hence the reference by hoteliers to the 'four-sevenths' nature of the business and their predilection for discounted weekend break offers, often worked up and marketed in

Table 2.4 Top 10 city tourism destinations in Europe by bednights generated in 2009

	Bednights (millions)	*Year-on performance (%)*
London	45.0	−6.0
Paris	33.9	−3.4
Berlin	18.9	+6.3
Rome	18.6	−2.6
Madrid	13.7	−1.6
Barcelona	12.8	+2.7
Prague	11.2	−7.7
Vienna	10.5	−4.2
Munich	9.9	+0.6
Amsterdam	8.6	+3.0

Source: ECM (2010)

conjunction with the CTO/CMO. The bedroom and bedspace occupancy profile by season typically shows troughs in demand occurring in high summer (when business demand drops off) and in winter, especially the post-New Year 'graveyard' months of January/February when both business and leisure tourism traffic is traditionally at its weakest. Occupancy profiles also vary markedly from one city to the next, so that in 2007, for instance, Barcelona and Paris registered bed occupancy levels of 80% and 78%, respectively, compared with Amsterdam and Munich where they were running at 59% and 57%, respectively. So, in that year Munich hotels were on average only just over half–full, whereas those in Barcelona were on average four-fifths full. Many cities report annual bed occupancy rates of less than 50%; in 2007, for example, the Austrian city of Bregenz recorded a striking low of just 13%, while Dubrovnik, Ghent, Venice and Rotterdam came out at 26%, 34%, 39% and 45%, respectively.

Crucially, bednights in conjunction with accommodation occupancy data provide quantitative evidence of the degree to which tourist capacity is being utilised, and how this is changing over time. For example, we can see in Figure 2.3 that hotel capacity in Vienna expanded by some 24% between 2003 and 2008, rising from 39,641 bedspaces to 49,005. This expansion occurred alongside steadily rising room occupancy levels – from a 2003 figure of 65% to 70% in 2008. In a nutshell, this reveals a 'best of both worlds' situation; a city significantly expanding its tourist capacity while more than maintaining accommodation utilisation levels. As well as charting tourist growth or decline over time, occupancy figures are valuable

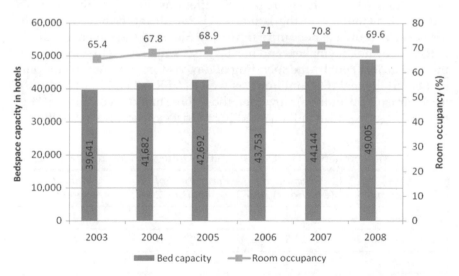

Figure 2.3 Room occupancy levels and bedspace capacity for Vienna, 2003–2008

'bellweather' indicators of a new trend. For instance, the effects of the 2009 economic recession could be quantified in Vienna by comparing, say, September 2009 achieved room occupancy levels of 72.6% with the average of 79.2% for the comparable period in 2008.

Measurement of Value: Community Measures

While trips, bednights and occupancy are key industry measures of performance by volume, it is tourist expenditure, income and jobs that measure value. *Tourist expenditure* is generally quantified by site and household surveys in which a range of sociodemographic data other than spending is sought. Table 2.5, for instance, draws on three national surveys to present expenditure data on the amount of UK tourism attributable to cities. It estimates that in gross terms city tourism was worth €57.8 billion in 2007, and that it formed 42%, 61% and 83% of domestic overnight, international overnight and day visitor spends, respectively. Table 2.5 also shows how in the United Kingdom the market share of city tourism has risen since the year 2000.

Tourist expenditure figures naturally vary widely between cities, reflecting size, accessibility and the strength and competitiveness of the business and leisure tourism 'offers'. In 2007, for instance, the small English cities of Exeter (population 122,000) and York (population 193,000) registered €61 million and €415 million, respectively compared with a figure of €648 million for Sheffield (population 534,000). The figures at first sight appear surprising in that York is widely recognised as a tourist destination, whereas fewer regard Sheffield as such, yet the statistics indicate that tourism in the latter city is worth more than it is in the former. The tourist expenditure figures in Sheffield, however, are dominated not by holidaymakers and heritage–seeking day excursionists (as is the case in York) but by the spending of day visitors coming for shopping and entertainment (€473 million), as well as VFR (€35 million) and business tourism (€49 million). Together, these three markets comprise 86% of the 2007 figure of €648 million cited for tourist expenditure in Sheffield.

Table 2.5 Market share of city tourism in the United Kingdom, 2000–2007

City tourism	Expenditure (€ billions) 2007	Percentage of all expenditure 2007	Market share ± since 2000
Domestic	9.6	42%	+4%
Overseas	12.8	61%	+4%
Day visits	35.4	83%	+1%

Source: The City Tourism Report (2009)

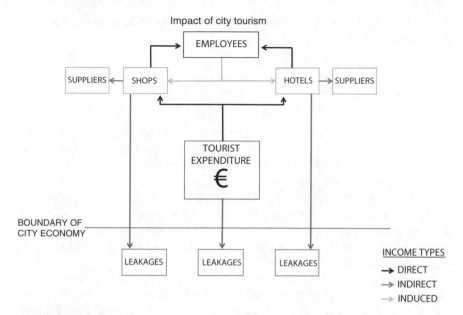

Figure 2.4 Multiplier effects of tourist expenditure in cities

Tourist expenditure statistics serve as a starting point on which to estimate the impact of tourism on the local economy in terms of *income* and *employment* generated. The measurement exercises here involve not only extensive survey work, but also sophisticated modelling as a basis for computations in the form of tourist multiplier studies. The aim is to quantify the impact of tourist expenditure as it works its way through the local economy, with successive rounds of spending and 'leakage'. Each spending round generates additional household income and jobs, the so-called direct, indirect and induced 'multiplier' effects of tourist expenditure as shown in Figure 2.4.

Figure 2.4 depicts and exemplifies these multiplier effects. The box in the centre is the estimated value of tourism expenditure. It might, for instance, be the €648 million and €415 million figures previously cited for Sheffield and York. As we can see from this diagram, some of the tourist expenditure leaks from the city economy while the remainder forms direct income to shops and hotels and their employees. Further income – this time what is referred to as indirect income – is generated as the hotels and shops purchase supplies locally. Yet more induced income arises as employees re-spend some of their income in the shops and restaurants and so it goes on until all of the initial injection of spending has worked its way out of the city economy. So, for the small English city of Canterbury, a tourist expenditure of €339 million was recorded in 2006, generating via the multiplier process:

- €321 million of direct income
- €64 million of indirect and induced income
- €385 million of local household income in total
- 5393 FTE jobs (some 13% of the local workforce)

The headline results from this impact study indicated a tourist multiplier effect of 1.2 in that the initial injection of tourist expenditure worth €339 million created in total €385 million of local income. Impact studies of this kind have a potentially powerful propaganda value and to an extent can help shape future policy. For example, the Canterbury figures demonstrated that only a small proportion of tourist expenditure found its way into the accommodation sector (some 12%) because the majority of visitors came only for the day. So, policy might be to promote only to overnight stay markets.

Measuring the multiplier effects of tourist expenditure on income and jobs itself comes at a financial cost (ca. €15,000 per annum to do it reasonably accurately), and it is essential for a CTO/CMA to make budgetary provision for this and other measurement exercises in order to monitor trends, inform advocacy and provide industry leadership. For a CTO/CMA, estimates of value in terms of expenditure, income and jobs are the essential community measures, and together with the industry measures previously described, there is a requirement on a continuous basis to research and report on them. Table 2.6, for instance, summarises the performance of Gothenburg's tourism economy over the 2002–2008 period, with a growth of 29%, 41% and 32%, respectively in bednights,

Table 2.6 Bednights, tourist expenditure and employment in Gothenburg 2002–2008

	Bednights ('000)	*Expenditure (€ million)*	*Employment (FTE jobs)*
2002	2580	1597	13,357
2003	2721	1813	15,000
2004	2729	1804	14,400
2005	2940	1882	15,200
2006	3050	2049	16,100
2007	3180	2156	16,900
2008	3320	2264	17,600

Source: Gothenburg & Co. (2009)

Table 2.7 Experience Nottinghamshire: Headline volume, value and impact figures 2003–2009

	2003	*2004*	*2005*	*2006*	*2007*	*2008*	*2009*
1	1219	1264	1374	1378	1437	TBA	TBA
2	21,622	21,576	22,547	22,132	22,476	TBA	TBA
3	4.1	4.1	4.3	4.6	4.8	TBA	TBA
4	256	259	288	310	331	TBA	TBA
5	N/A	N/A	N/A	63	64	86	58*

1 Day and staying visitor expenditure in Nottinghamshire (€m)
2 Number of FTE jobs
3 Number of staying visitors using commercial accommodation (millions)
4 Discretionary spending of staying visitors using commercial accommodation (€m)
5 Percentage room occupancy
*Year-to-date figure (comparable year-to-date figure for 2008 was 64%)
Source: Experience Nottinghamshire (March 2009)

expenditure and employment when 2002 is compared with 2008. As Chief Executive of Experience Nottinghamshire between 2004 and 2009 (see Chapter 5), the author was responsible to a board of directors representing local authorities, universities, colleges and local businesses. A standard item at every board meeting was the latest volume, value and accommodation occupancy statistics, and the reporting format is shown in Table 2.7. In many respects, the most important line was the fourth one – the one labelled 'discretionary spending of staying visitors using commercial accommodation'. In this respect, Table 2.7 indicates that the figures drawn from the tourist multiplier studies carried out each year recorded impressive year-on growth in real terms – from €256 million in 2003 to €331 million in 2007. In turn, this provided 'hard' quantitative evidence that Experience Nottinghamshire was performing well and otherwise doing 'a good job'.

Measurement of Marketing Effectiveness: Marketing Measures

The industry and community measures we have so far considered differ from measures of marketing effectiveness. Reflecting on city tourist organisation – and for that matter regional and national tourist organisation – I think it is fair to say that measures of marketing effectiveness have not traditionally been a strong point. There has been a tendency to report lots of marketing, but key performance indicators (KPIs) and rate of return on investment (ROI) calculations have until lately been conspicuous by their absence. As such, the practice of destination marketing at national, regional and local levels has been criticised for being vague and indeterminate, and lacking in rigour – there has been a kind of 'never mind the quality, feel the width of this brochure' approach.

Over the past few years, *marketing evaluation* studies have become much more common, to the point where at Experience Nottinghamshire they were routinely a part of every marketing campaign being undertaken. The studies themselves were commissioned from external and therefore independent research agencies, at a cost of approximately €4000 per campaign. I will illustrate what was involved by referring to a specific study: the evaluation study for the 'Explore Nottingham, Discover Christmas' 2008 marketing campaign. This campaign targeted day visitors. The study was based on a sample of nearly 5000 respondents who in response to the campaign had either been sent a brochure or had visited a bespoke website. The respondents were invited by email to complete an online questionnaire to determine the extent to which they had been influenced by the campaign. There was a 40% 'gross' conversion rate – in other words, 40% of the sample responded to the campaign by visiting Nottingham. This became an 18% 'net' conversion rate when the so-called weighting adjustments were made; 'definites', people who said they definitely visited because of the campaign, were given a value of 1.0; 'probables' a value of 0.5 and 'possibles' a value of 0.25. The net conversion rate of 18% produced an ROI of 5.6; meaning that for every €1 of marketing expenditure or investment, €5.60 of visitor spend was created. From this it was possible in a clear and evidenced way to establish that the campaign cost of €45,000 brought about a return to the local economy of €253,000 of additional visitor spend. Interim performance assessment of the campaign was possible through KPIs such as visits to the campaign website. Three observations are worth making about marketing evaluation studies.

Firstly, ROI calculations are only as good as the extent to which the sample mirrors the audiences being targeted. This is achievable, but great care must be taken to ensure that the external research agency devises a sample which is representative. Secondly, in addition to providing precise measures of conversion and ROI, marketing evaluation studies also provide valuable market intelligence on length of stay, activities undertaken, perceptions and likes and dislikes. Furthermore, the online surveys enable a profile to be assembled of potential customers who were exposed to the campaign, but in the event had decided not to visit. From this it is possible to ascertain whether the reasons for not visiting were related to the campaign itself and/or were attributable instead to the weakness of the product on offer.

Third, the ROI calculations give you 'nowhere to hide' as the chief executive of a CTO/CMA! To say the least, it is very embarrassing to receive and report on a poor ROI. However, though the results may prove uncomfortable, few would disagree that marketing evaluation studies are a considerable step forward, enabling the marketing activities of

Table 2.8 Convention bureaux performance data 2006: Barcelona, Brussels, Copenhagen and Geneva

	Convention bureau		MICE sector for destination				Convention bureau marketing					
	Budget (€ millions)	Staff	Meetings	Number of delegates ('000)	Overnight stays (millions)	Value (€ millions)	Meetings	Number of delegates ('000)	Overnight stays (millions)	Value (€ millions)	Convention bureau share of value (%)	ROI
Barcelona	1.6	9	1303	491	1.7	919	84	57	0.6	96	10	60
Brussels	1.6	9	–	–	1.7	–	128	52	0.9	29	–	18
Copenhagen	4.5	12	–	–	3.0	1000	165	53	0.2	70	14	15
Geneva	0.8	8	1400	500	0.9	1000	65	53	0.1	40	25	50

Source: ECM (2007)

CTOs/CMAs to be measured and made accountable, giving stakeholders vital indicators of performance and 'payback'. They are the essential marketing measures.

In relation specifically to business tourism, the nature of the marketing undertaken enables even more precise tracking of 'leads' as these are converted by the CTO/CMA into conference sales. In this respect, Table 2.8 compares the performance (in 2006) of four leading European convention bureaux – those for Barcelona, Brussels, Copenhagen and Geneva. Bureau budgets range from €0.80 to €4.5, while the economic contributions of the business tourism or MICE sector as a whole (meetings, incentives, conferences and exhibitions) pans out for each of the cities at around the €1 billion mark annually. The number of business tourism meetings directly attributable to bureaux marketing and the associated delegate numbers, overnight stays and economic value is presented in Table 2.8. This indicates (a) a convention bureau 'share' of between 10% and 25% of the local MICE sector and (b) impressive ROI values of between 15 and 60.

Intercity Comparison: Benchmarking

Unfortunately, benchmarking is not undertaken extensively in respect of the three sets of measures we have considered above – industry, community and marketing. This generalisation applies locally, regionally, nationally and internationally. Some progress has been made on a pan-European basis by European Cities Marketing, especially in respect of benchmarking by bednights (European Cities Marketing, 2009). At a city level, benchmarking by bednights and other measures is occasionally undertaken, as we have seen in Figure 2.2 which shows how Berlin Tourism compares its bednight statistics with those of other leading German cities. As a broad generalisation, knowledge sharing in the form of intercity benchmarking represents a considerable challenge, and for this reason practice is at present selective and fitful. There are three main considerations to bear in mind. Firstly, across regions and nations there is a lack of complete and comparable data. Secondly, there is a sense in which city tourism organisation is inherently local in outlook so that benchmarking does not come naturally and easily. Thirdly, CTOs/CMAs are operationally driven, so that benchmarking all too often becomes a low priority, like so much of the research and intelligence gathering of which it is a part. So, presently benchmarking is very much 'work in progress' and a challenge for all involved in city marketing.

Conclusions

Accurately measuring impacts from city tourism and the marketing with which it is associated is fundamental. CTOs/CMAs must make these assessments in order to monitor trends and performance, and to quantify stakeholder 'payback'. A really critical factor is to gauge the success or otherwise of a CTO/CMA in putting 'heads in beds'; especially in growing discretionary overnight stay tourism across business and leisure tourism markets. It is important to have all four sets of measurement vehicles in place – the industry measures, the community ones, the potentially embarrassing marketing evaluation studies, and the intercity benchmarking. As we have seen, this raises important cost, 'cultural' and data comparability issues, but we should 'grasp the nettle' here because – to remind ourselves once again of Drucker's erstwhile maxim – 'if you can't measure it, you can't manage it'.

Chapter 3

The Dynamics of City Tourism

Introduction

European city tourism organisation has its public and private sector components. This has always been the way of things, as detailed in several excellent historical texts (e.g. Neale, 1981) and in more contemporary accounts (e.g. Elliott, 1997). There is inevitability about the involvement of both sectors – even if there are shifts of emphasis over time, as well as significant variations between and within nation states. As a generality, however, private bodies are central to the provision of hospitality, transport and entertainment services, and they also support the marketing of cities, as can be seen, for instance, with tour operators and airlines. Public sector intervention is brought about by a variety of factors, foremost amongst which are the requirements to regulate private sector activities, to provide non-remunerative infrastructure and superstructure, to remove obstacles to more effective private sector performance and to redress market failures. The four modes of intervention gain diverse expression – from portal websites, coach parks, toilets, road improvement schemes, convention centres and tourist police, through to signage, visitor guides, the licensing of taxis, training schemes and lighting. Even mortuary accommodation and graveyards can be geared to the requirements of the local tourism industry (Heeley, 1980b).

Over and above intervention, the rationale for public sector involvement in city tourism has another important dimension, that of leadership and coordination. For in every city, large or small, there is an administrative conundrum. The tourism sector is fragmented, being dominated by small- to medium-sized enterprises, and it is ill-defined inasmuch as the majority of services provided by the public and private sectors do not depend solely on tourism – they are consumed by residents, students, non-tourism businesses and other interests. A chronic need therefore exists for some or other organisational mechanism to represent, coordinate and advance the interests of the city's tourism sector. This exigency, allied to the need to market the place as an entity, provides the twin rationale for the emergence of city tourism organisation.

As we have seen in Chapter 1, CTOs and CMAs are increasingly constituted as a 'hybrid' of the local public and private sector; partnerships constituted, managed and funded as more or less independent agencies to exercise the classic leadership and coordination roles referred to above. Where the independence of the CTO/CMA is more rather than less, then the partnership is premised on the public sector 'letting go' of some of its traditional intervention and leadership accountabilities. Crucially, in 'letting go', the local public sector as represented by the city government will demand the participation – financial and otherwise – of other key players and stakeholders, especially the local private sector as represented by small and medium enterprises (SMEs) as well as larger local companies and institutions. A critical ratio is the extent to which the municipal grant is matched by other income streams, referred to as leverage. In the remainder of this chapter, we shall exemplify how CTOs/CMAs working 'hand in glove' with a supportive municipal authority have in the most unpropitious of circumstances been able to engineer for their respective cities a buoyant tourism sector and a vibrant 21st century image.

Five City Tourism Success Stories

The following five 'mini' case studies span the late 20th and early 21st centuries, and mirror a period of low-cost travel, ambitious urban regeneration schemes, of mushrooming city break and convention markets, of ever more intense competition for 'footloose' sporting and cultural events, as well as new ways of working brought about by partnership of the public and private sector and by the web and internet. The accounts below recount the experience of one capital and four so-called 'second' cities, as they have sought to position themselves nationally and globally, and to secure self-sustaining growth of their local tourist sectors. As we shall see, each city in its own way has been demonstrably innovative and successful.

Case Study 1: Glasgow 1983–2010

Glasgow is Scotland's largest city (population 581,000) and suffers from a negative image, based largely on past violence and deprivation, as famously depicted in the novel *No Mean City* first published in 1935. Written by an unemployed Glaswegian and a London journalist, its anti-hero was the razor-wielding Johnnie Stark. Serious scarcity, scarring and economic decline continued to characterise Glasgow in the post-war period, manifested in the rationalisation of engineering and shipbuilding, much substandard housing and environment, and high levels of unemployment and out-migration. Indeed, Glasgow's diaspora provided the basis for early, municipal-led tourist promotions, culminating in the 1983 'Welcome Home to Glasgow' marketing campaign. The latter was perforce low key. Tourism was not a priority. The city had just 3000 hotel rooms, its tourist information centre was a 'temporary' 25-year-old hut situated in George Square, and awaiting the visitor, there was a limited and 'underwhelming' range of visitor attractions. This situation was to be improved significantly by the opening late in 1983 of the €20.3 million *Burrell Collection*. This attraction enabled the city's stock of municipal cultural assets, particularly its museums and art galleries, to be offered realistically on the tourist marketplace. It also gave impetus to the *Glasgow's miles better* public relations campaign which, commencing in 1983 and very much the inspiration of the Lord Provost of Glasgow Council, sought to foster positive images of the city as an antidote to the prevailing negative ones.

The establishment of the Greater Glasgow Tourist Board (GGTB) in 1983 marked the start of a long-term, proactive and coordinated approach to destination marketing and development, involving key players across the public and private sectors (Heeley, 1986). Under its persuasive, fast-talking Chief Executive, Eddie Friel, and with strong support from the political leadership of Glasgow District Council, GGTB went energetically about the tasks of promoting and advertising the city, and servicing the information requirements of those arriving there. On the back of a study of Glasgow's tourism potential completed in 1983 by the consultants Panel Kerr Foster, GGTB was also to play a supporting role in attracting flagship cultural and sporting events to the city and in encouraging new hotel and attractions developments, working in conjunction with Glasgow District Council and the Scottish Development Agency. The outcomes over a near 30-year period have been little short of sensational. International tourists to Glasgow in 2008 numbered 4,280,000. By then, the city's hotel capacity had more than trebled, and there were now 10 first-class visitor attractions attracting in excess of 4 million admissions (see Table 3.1). Tourism in 2008 accounted for 31,000 FTE jobs, some 7.9% of the local workforce. As Eddie Friel was quick to point out, this was more than had ever been employed in the city's once former staple industry of shipbuilding. Glasgow's current tourism strategy celebrates it having become over this period 'one of the UK's foremost destinations for festivals and cultural events ... particularly successful in winning and staging major sporting events of a national and international stature over the past twenty years' (Glasgow Marketing Bureau, 2006: 23).

Back in 1983, GGTB itself had been constituted as a company limited by guarantee, and for the 1985/1986 year it worked to a budget of €550,000. In that year, the bulk of this income (82%) was derived from local authority grant, with the remainder coming from the national tourist board (14%) and commercial membership fees (4%). Despite the then proportionately low financial stake of the private sector, it comprised nearly half (12) of the 25-member executive committee which governed the work of GGTB.

Table 3.1 Admissions to Glasgow visitor attractions 2008

	Admissions ('000)
Kelvingrove Art Gallery and Museum	1445
Gallery of Modern Art	563
Glasgow Science Centre	481
Museum of Transport	456
Botanical Gardens	400
People's Palace	252
Burrell Collection	203
Centre for Contemporary Arts	186
Glasgow Cathedral	153
St Mungo Museum of Religious Life and Art	152

Source: Visit Scotland (2009)

Twelve of the remaining committee members represented the local author-ities, and the final member was a nominee of the national tourist board (namely the Scottish Tourist Board, subsequently Visit Scotland). Reflecting as it did a wide range of private and public sector tourism interests, GGTB was able to act as a centralised marketing mechanism and over time levered increased financial resources from non-local authority sources. It also assumed the critical leadership and coordination role to which we have referred at the beginning of this chapter. The latter was exemplified in 1986 when opposition by Glasgow hoteliers to plans for a new on-site hotel at the *Scottish Exhibition and Conference Centre* was transformed into support after GGTB mediation. The centre itself was opened in 1985 at a capital cost of €40.3 million on the site of the former Queen's Dock. A prime symbol of Glasgow's aspiration to reinvent itself as a post-industrial city, the Centre's 2000-seater auditorium and supporting facilities made it Scotland's foremost meetings and exhibition venue. The greater part of the capital funding for this project (78%) was shared equally by the national government and the local authorities, with the private sector footing the remaining 22%. With respect to conventions marketing, GGTB made out a case to Glasgow District Council in 1986 for additional funding to enable it to penetrate national association and international meetings segments, and in the following year a business tourism department was established which would introduce – as we shall see later – a highly successful confer-ence ambassador scheme (Friel, 1989).

Directly opposite the Scottish Exhibition and Conference Centre lay the former Princess Dock, the site of the *1988 Glasgow Garden Festival*.

This event was funded entirely by the national government and attracted 4.25 million visitors, well ahead of the 3 million target and the figures achieved at previous festivals in Liverpool and Stoke. It performed less well in financial terms, with the gross cost of €45.9 million offset by visitor revenues and other income, to leave a net cost of €20.2 million, over double the original projection of €9.5 million. That said, the Festival marked a significant step in Glasgow's development as a city tourism destination (Heeley & Pearlman, 1988). Alongside the city's designation as the *1990 European Capital of Culture* and annual festivals such as Mayfest and Glasgow International Jazz, it illustrated the city's events-led tourism strategy. In the absence of major permanent visitor attractions, the twin aims of the strategy were (1) to use events in order to improve Glasgow's image and to persuade tourists to visit the city and (2) to strive in the meantime to develop permanent new visitor attractions. A start had been made with the Burrell Collection, and in the 1990s there followed the *Glasgow Royal Concert Hall* (1991), a revamping and resiting of the *Glasgow Museum of Transport*, as well as the building of the *St Mungo Museum of Religious Life and Art* (1993) and the *Glasgow Gallery of Modern Art* (1996).

Significantly, the GGTB had led a successful bid to host European Capital of Culture in 1990, beating off competition from the Scottish capital, Edinburgh! By 2003, the Board's income had risen sevenfold from what it had been in 1983, standing at €3.9 million. Its annual report for 2002/2003 pointed to a string of events hosted by the city and to the resultant economic impact – including the 2002 UEFA Champion's League Final. The report also referred to GGTB's pioneering conference ambassador scheme which enlisted the support of locally based academics, scientists, doctors and businessmen – mostly based at the city's three universities. The ambassadors were encouraged to 'bring home' to Glasgow prestigious meetings with which they were associated. GGTB supported the ambassadors with bid preparation for the event and with its subsequent hosting. By 2003, GGTB's Director of Marketing reported that the scheme had been instrumental in winning the following events: the 2004 Annual Congress of the European Respiratory Society; the 2005 European Optical Communications conference; the 2005 World Science Fiction Convention; the 2006 International Congress on Parisitology; and the 2008 International Congress of Midwives. Three years later, the army of 2300 ambassadors networked under the scheme had secured in the 2005/2006 year no less than 89 conferences with an estimated delegate spend of €15.6 million to be injected into the local economy. The city's conference facilities were soon to be boosted by a Sir Norman Foster designed extension to the Scottish Exhibition and Conference Centre in the shape of the 3000 seater *Clyde Auditorium* (1997).

In 1999, Glasgow celebrated its hosting of the UK City of Architecture and Design – a designation it had achieved in the face of competition from Edinburgh and Liverpool – with the opening of the Lighthouse arts complex. Further investment in tourism superstructure in 2001 took the form of the *Glasgow Centre for Contemporary Art* and the *Glasgow Science Centre*. Built at a cost of €84 million and situated next door to the Scottish Exhibition and Conference Centre, the Science Centre is currently attracting nearly half a million paid visitor admissions a year (refer Table 3.1), combining exhibitory with an IMAX. Into the present century, the sustained development of tourist superstructure was exemplified by the €31.1 million three-year refurbishment (2004–2006) of the *Kelvingrove Art Gallery and Museum* and in plans for what will become Europe's largest indoor sports arena and velodrome. The latter facility will enable Glasgow to host the *2014 Commonwealth Games* at a projected capital cost estimated at €130 million.

From 2004 onwards, GGTB spearheaded the implementation of a bold and well-resourced city brand project titled *Glasgow: Scotland with style* – see Chapter 7. The development of the brand had been masterminded by the Board's founder Chief Executive, Eddie Friel. Its launch in 2004 provoked mixed media coverage, and in the event, Friel was to leave his post later on in that year when confronted with a controversial reorganisation of Scottish tourism administration which sought increased centralisation of destination marketing functions through the national tourist organisation, Visit Scotland. The CMA was restructured in 2005, renaming itself the *Glasgow Marketing Bureau*. It compensated for the loss of its visitor serving functions to Visit Scotland with the acquisition of enhanced capabilities in respect of sourcing, attracting and hosting 'footloose' sporting and cultural events. In retaining its separate existence, the new Bureau effectively asserted its right to market the city region independently of Visit Scotland.

The Glasgow Marketing Bureau currently has 43 staff, its Chairman is the Leader of Glasgow District Council, and its principal operational activities are custodianship of the city brand, tourism marketing campaigns across city breaks and conventions, and media relations. It works to a 10-year strategy on behalf of its principal public and private stakeholders. The story it symbolises, and which it has done much to bring about, is a truly remarkable one. In Bill Bryson's classic travel book *Notes from a Small Island*, the author recalled a first visit to Glasgow in 1973: 'I had never seen a place so choked and grubby. Everywhere seemed black and cheerless. Even the local accent seemed born of clinkers and grit …. And there were no tourists – none at all. Glasgow may be the largest city in Scotland, but my *Let's Go* guide to Europe didn't even mention it' (Bryson, 1995: 338). There is little exaggeration contained in Bryson's description of 1970's Glasgow. Nowadays, as former tourist chief Eddie

Friel said recently in a newspaper profile, the 'place is absolutely on a roll … Glasgow is a dynamic, modern, European city'.

Case Study 2: Barcelona 1986–2010

The Catalonian capital of Barcelona (population 1.6 million) rose to prominence in the 19th century to become Spain's leading manufacturing centre, its hallmark and industrial staple being the production of textiles and related machinery. Although the city had staged prestigious events throughout its long history – notably the Universal Exhibition (1888), the International Exhibition (1929), the Eucharistic Congress (1952) and the World Cup (1982), its tourism potential went largely unrecognised and underexploited until the last decade of the 20th century. This reflected the country's turbulent 20th-century history and, specifically, the Spanish Civil War (1936–1939) and the oppressive dictatorship which followed in its wake. Spain's gradual transition to democracy from 1975 onwards, and the designation in 1986 of Barcelona as the host city for the 1992 Olympic Games mark the starting points for an impressive development of the tourism sector and for the city's post-industrial reinvention. Notwithstanding the serious impact of the current economic recession, the city's unenviable reputation for tourist theft, and recent setbacks – the return to Berlin of the twice-yearly Bread and Butter fashion trade show, as well as the murder of Félix Martínez Touriño, the Director of the Barcelona Convention Centre – there can be no doubting the tremendous progress made by the Catalonian capital throughout the past two decades. Over a 14-year period (1986–2000) Barcelona's conversion into a 'must see' city on the European tourist map manifested itself in a trebling of Barcelona's hotel capacity and a doubling in the number of international visitors. As Table 2.2 in Chapter 2 demonstrates, this growth continued into the current decade to the point where in 2006 – incredibly from the vantage point of the Civil War and the Franco dictatorship – Barcelona had become the fifth most-visited city in Europe and Spain's most popular tourist destination.

Returning to our starting point, Barcelona in 1986 was awarded the 25th *Olympic Games*, beating off competition from Amsterdam, Belgrade, Birmingham, Brisbane and Paris. Relative to the previous summer Olympics, its hosting of the event in 1992 was a great success in organisational and sporting terms, providing an immediate boost to the external image of the city. A noteworthy feature of the 1992 Games was that public–private partnership was strongly evident; especially in the joint venture arrangement which spearheaded the main capital works (€5.4 billion). In addition, a much higher proportion (75%) of the revenue/organisational costs (€915 million) than previously was recouped from sponsorship and television rights. The points to emphasise with respect to the capital costs

were the scale and long-term value of the infrastructure and superstructure developments completed. The principal investments were in venues,
in transport, in a spruced-up city centre, and in the rehabilitation of two
areas; the obsolete and run-down harbour area around Port Vell at the foot
of the Ramblas, and the disintegrating industrial district of Poble Nou
which was transformed to become the Olympic village and marina. What
we would now refer to as 'legacy' effects of the 1992 Games were profound, as the city harnessed the Olympic impetus and investments to
create sustained tourist growth and to fashion a new image for Barcelona:
an identity characterised by urbanism, culture and style. In a nutshell, the
Olympic legacy formed a platform on which the city was able to showcase
its unique heritage, its independence and regional Catalonian identity, its
Mediterranean climate and beaches, and its distinctive cultural and architectural achievements as epitomised in the works of Picasso, Miró and
Gaudi. This was done so effectively that successful urban regeneration
linked to major events has become known as the *Barcelona model*.

Securing the nomination for the Olympics in 1986 instituted a 'process
of critical reflection on the city … and in particular of its role as a tourist
centre' (Duran, 2005: 4). This manifested itself from 1987 onwards in regular meetings between the Barcelona Municipal Council and the Barcelona
Chamber of Commerce, Industry and Shipping. The aim of these meetings
was that there should be a systematic, planned approach to exploit the
city's tourism potential. A comprehensive audit was undertaken and this,
in turn, paved the way for the preparation of the Barcelona Strategic
Tourism Plan, culminating in the establishment of the plan's delivery
mechanism – *Barcelona Tourism* – in 1993. This CTO was constituted as a
public–private consortium and made responsible for destination marketing and for keeping under continuous review the city's tourism strategy.
Governance was discharged through a General Council and a supporting
Executive Committee, headed, respectively, by the Mayor of Barcelona
and the President of the Chamber of Commerce, Industry and Shipping.
Other members of the Council and Committee were nominees of Barcelona
Municipal Council and the Chamber. The day-to-day involvement of the
private sector was captured through commercial members drawn from
the ranks of the tourist trade, namely shops, accommodation, catering,
visitor attractions, meetings venues and transport operators. Guided by
its General Manager, Pere Duran i Vall Llossera, Barcelona Tourism in
2008 had no less than 676 private sector members, nearly half of whom
were a part of the consortium's convention bureau department (Barcelona
Tourism, 2008). Over the years, Barcelona Tourism built up formidable
amounts of trading and other earned income on the back of two core
funding grants from the Council and Chamber: in 1994 the majority of the
CTO's €4.1 million budget came from these two grants (54%); by 2008 a
striking 93% of its €30.7 million income derived from earned income

streams. In that year, sales from the TIC network and tourist bus services accounted for 81% of the gross earned income total of €28 million.

The *1993 Barcelona Strategic Tourism Plan* signalled a move from the so-called 'generic' destination marketing to tactical campaigns targeting eight main market segments, namely meetings, culture, shopping, cruises, sport, gastronomy, gay and health. The resultant growth in leisure and business tourism to Barcelona has been spectacular, as summarised by the various indicators set out in Table 3.2. A telling feature is that while the capacity of the hotel sector as measured by bedspaces expanded by 182% during 1990–2006, the bednights recorded from those staying overnight rose by 221%, producing a more or less consistent trend of high but steadily rising occupancy levels. A more even balance of tourists across business and leisure purposes became evident, with leisure tourism accounting for 49% of all staying trips in 2006, compared to 24% in 1990.

By its very nature, the 'Barcelona model' has meant that the city's tourist growth has been closely linked to the staging of major sporting, cultural and business events. As well as annual festivals such as *Grec* – a summer showcasing of dance, theatre and music first held in 1976 – and *Sonar* (1993 onwards) with its cutting-edge electronic media and multimedia, there has been a series of 'one-off' productions, ranging from the Miró Year (1993), Gaudi Year (2002), the Universal Forum of Culture (2004), the Year of Gastronomy (2005), through to Picasso Barcelona (2006) and the World Architecture Festival (2009). In their turn, these events have complimented and utilised the city's renowned architecture, its old town and its established cultural facilities, notably the *Opera House* (1847) and a clutch of pre-Olympic attractions which together generate annually in the region

Table 3.2 Indicators of tourism growth in Barcelona, 1990 compared with 2006

	1990	*2006*	*% change*
No. of hotels	118	285	+141
No. of bedspaces	18,569	52,484	+182
Room occupancy	71%	78%	+7
No. of staying tourists	1,732,902	7,109,808	+318
No. of bednights	3,795,522	12,202,105	+221
No. of meetings delegates	105,000	491,000	+468
No. of cruises	132,807	1,400,000	+950
No. of airport passengers	9,000,000	30,000,000	+233

Source: Barcelona Tourism (2007)

of 7 million paid admissions, namely *Barcelona Zoo* (1892), the *Spanish Village* (1929), Gaudi's *Sagrada Familia* (his famous unfinished church) and his La *Pedrera* (designed originally as a modern apartment block), as well as the *Picasso Museum* (1963), *Miro Foundation* (1975) and the *FC Barcelona Museum* at Camp Nou (1984). To this rich base of visitor attractions, there have been added new post-Olympic draws, for example the *Centre of Contemporary Culture* (1994), the *Museum of Contemporary Art* (1995), the *Museum of Catalan Art* (1990), the *National Theatre of Catalonia* (1997), the *Aquarium* and the *Maremagnum* leisure shopping complex. As for sport, the legacy of Olympic venues made possible the introduction of an annual programme of events, taking place at more or less the same time each year – from hockey in January to the Barcelona Marathon in March and Barcelona Polo Classic in May, through to the Jean Boulin Race in December. Supplementing this, there has been a regular diet of high-profile 'one-off' championships such as the 2000 Davis Cup, and those staged for World Swimming and European Hockey in 2003. In 2010, Barcelona will be the setting for the European Athletics Championship.

Finally, the infrastructure constructed for the 1992 Games made possible the staging of large-scale meetings and exhibitions. In particular, Barcelona positioned itself on the international car industry circuit as a prime location for new model launches, and during 1993–2001 no fewer than 127 major automobile-related events took place in the city. For instance, in 1999, a total of 12,900 delegates attended three product launches for Toyota, Saab and Volkswagen. In the immediate aftermath of the Games, Barcelona hosted the prestigious annual conference of the International Union of Architects (UIA) at the Palau Sant Jordi – the multipurpose arena and events venue built for the 1992 Olympics. The World Congress of Rotary Clubs was staged in the same venue in 2002. The opening of the *Barcelona International Convention Centre* (2004) cemented the city's position as a premier league meetings destination and by 2006 it occupied fourth place in the International Congress and Convention Association (ICCA) world rankings, behind Vienna, Paris and Singapore. The new convention centre boasts of 1000 m² of flexible, sea-facing exhibition and conference space, and in its first two years of operation was the setting for the World Conference on Lung Cancer, the International Rail Forum and the World Conference of the Association of Corporate Travel Executives (ACTE). In 2007, Barcelona hosted an estimated 340 association meetings and 1435 corporate events, with a resultant influx of 630,000 delegates – 83% higher than that recorded in 1990 (Garrigosa, 2008). Delegates to these events spent an estimated €1.7 billion. The contribution made by Barcelona Tourism via its convention department is shown in Table 2.7 of Chapter 2.

George Orwell (1982: 9), writing about Barcelona in *Homage to Catalonia* at the time of the Spanish Civil War, referred to the ubiquitous flags, destroyed churches, collectivised shops and restaurants, the 'evil atmosphere of war', and the city's 'gaunt untidy look'. Half-a-century later, the city hosted a spectacularly successful Summer Olympics, providing the touchstone over the next two decades for its event-led reinvention as a city. It has become a role model of urban regeneration, one of Europe's most visited cities, and as one travel writer summed it up, 'a global trademark of refined urban life, advanced design, and Mediterranean hedonism'.

Case Study 3: Birmingham 1976–2010

Birmingham Convention and Visitor Bureau (BCVB) was set up in 1982 in order to capitalise on investments in the National Exhibition Centre (NEC). Funded and underwritten by Europe's largest local authority, Birmingham City Council, the NEC itself had been opened in 1976. Its location on the outskirts of Birmingham (population 1,004,000) was controversial; partly because a national facility had been built close to 'Brum' – a provincial, unfashionable and rather unloved city – but also due to a widespread fear that promoters and organisers would be reluctant to move their 'shows' to the Midlands. Such fears proved unwarranted; the first event to be staged there was the International Spring Fair, and others quickly followed; amongst them were the high-profile British International Motor Show, Crufts (the world's largest dog show), the annual conference of the Confederation of British Industry and the Horse of the Year Show. BCVB's initial preoccupation was to service these and other major events attracted to the Centre, supplying information to delegates from its NEC offices and – all importantly – providing event organisers with a bespoke accommodation booking service in which often complex and demanding specifications would be matched against the available capacity and facilities. Alongside this core business and guided by its founder Chief Executive, Philippe Taylor, BCVB spread its wings into Birmingham proper, becoming England's first major CTO, promoting the city's short-break offers and operating TIC services in the city centre.

BCVB's short break and visitor servicing activities were to receive a tremendous fillip in the last decade of the 20th century as Birmingham's dull, confusing, and in parts unsightly city centre underwent a breathtaking transformation, in line with the recommendations contained in the 1990 City Centre Urban Design Study. This set out to create a traffic-and-barrier-free environment, topped off by a trio of impressive public squares – Victoria, Chamberlain and Centenary. At the far end of the latter square, a visionary €300 million development opened in 1991, comprising the International Convention Centre (ICC), the National Indoor Arena (NIA) and the Birmingham Symphony Hall (BSH). Managed and marketed by what had now become the NEC Group, Birmingham capitalised fully on these new facilities and the now well-established National Exhibition

Centre, and was soon able to take up a dominating plus 40% share of the United Kingdom's entire conference and exhibition trade. In the decade following their 1991 openings, the ICC/NIA/BSH complex was to be the catalyst for the private sector-led development of a 'convention quarter', comprising 3000 hotel rooms and over 250 licensed premises located in the adjacent Broad Street and canal ways. In the 1990s, there was real substance to the argument that tourism and leisure might reinvent 'Brum' in the wake of the dramatic decline and rationalisation of its metal manufacturing and motor car industries in the previous decade.

In tandem with the contemporary, 'chic', and metropolitan Birmingham which was emerging Phoenix like in the 1990s, the city reorganised the way it promoted itself. This followed a review by a television reporter turned consultant, Vincent Hanna. His report declared that the manner in which the city was promoting itself was 'gauche and provincial', lampooning the City Council's V-shaped logo and calling for a more confident and modern approach to communicating the city's assets to the outside world (Hanna, 1992). A key element of the new approach was that it should be apolitical; while Birmingham City Council needed to be financially supportive, it should at the same time be at arm's length. In 1993, as a consequence of the review, BCVB was incorporated into a new venture – the *Birmingham Marketing Partnership* (BMP). The partnership came under the stewardship of a new Chief Executive, Michael Thorley and – reflecting the massive and brave NEC Group investments – it became custodian of a city brand whose ambitious strapline was *'Birmingham: Europe's meeting place'*. In 1998, a striking demonstration of this motto occurred when in the space of two months the city hosted the Lions Club International Convention (reputedly the world's largest meeting), the G8 summit and the Eurovision Song Contest. The latter event was televised from the Birmingham National Indoor Arena to a worldwide audience in excess of 300 million. Working together, the NEC Group, BMP and the City Council's Communications Department had sourced, bid for and then successfully delivered all three of these flagship events. City leaders and tourist chief were justly triumphant and valedictory.

BMP combined within a single organisation tourism and city image/ promotion roles – what we have classified in Chapter 1 as a CMA. This mirrored an organisational trend which would come to characterise England in the rest of the decade (see Chapter 1). In the Birmingham case, however, the advent of BMP, and the associated bolting together of tourism and city promotion/image programmes was not accompanied by their crystallisation into a purposeful, coherent and coordinated set of marketing activities. By the new millennium, it was clear that further restructuring was required, not only to address this problem, but several others. IT was antiquated, office environments were poor, strategy and performance planning arrangements were not in place and proactive commercial approaches were as rare as sales capabilities and accountabilities. Confusingly and irrationally, the Economic Development Department of Birmingham City Council had latterly established a five strong Tourism Team outside of the BMP structure. The received wisdom was that BMP never regained the momentum of 1998, and by the new Millennium had simply 'fallen behind the times' (Braun, 2008: 125).

In response to this situation, a new BMP Chief Executive (the author) was recruited early in 2001 to reorganise and strengthen how the city promoted itself. This led to the winding up of the Partnership and to the establishment of *Marketing Birmingham*. How Birmingham might promote itself was outlined in a paper which I presented to the relevant stakeholders in October 2001, and this included the integration and co-location of the Council's Tourism Team within the new structure. Marketing Birmingham as an organisation was formally incorporated on 24 April 2002, moving 7 months later into 8000 sq. ft of prestigious office space set within the city's new €112 million Millennium Point complex. In the following year, the company's accommodation booking service serviced the exacting requirements of a huge textile exhibition known as International Textiles Machinery Association (ITMA), and in the same year there were the openings of what were to become award-winning tourism centres at the Rotunda and in Birmingham New Street. By then, Marketing Birmingham was implementing a new place brand – the *'Birmingham b'* – and it was in receipt of a massive €3.5 million European Regional Development Fund (ERDF) award to equip the organisation with state-of-the-art IT. Indeed, the 2002 launch prospectus for Marketing Birmingham boasted that it was set to become the best-resourced and most-integrated destination marketing organisation in England (Marketing Birmingham, 2002). By the 2004/2005 financial year, this was indeed the case, with the company's annual budget standing at over €7 million. (The comparable BMP 2001/2002 figure was €2.6 million.) Two key elements of Marketing Birmingham's 2003/2004 budget were a revamped commercial membership scheme and a pioneering corporate citizenship project – Championing Birmingham. In 2003/2004, Championing Birmingham brought in €670,000 of private sector donations and other funding.

I left Birmingham in October 2003, and the company recruited a new Chairman and Chief Executive in the following year. Since 2004, Marketing Birmingham has consolidated its position as one of the United Kingdom's leading CMAs. Between 2004 and 2008, the number of tourists visiting the city annually rose from 29 million to more than 32 million, and hotel bedstock expanded by some 9%. For 2008/2009, fees from the company's commercial membership scheme and donations from its now 44 Championing Birmingham supporters grossed €1.5 million. There is a strong ongoing financial commitment on the part of Birmingham City Council. For the 2009/2010 financial year, Marketing Birmingham's budgeted income stood at an impressive €10.2 million, although there is arguably too heavy a reliance on public sources of funding (85%). Major events, meetings and exhibitions continue to contribute significantly to the city economy. The 100th Annual Rotary International Convention held at the NEC in June 2009 attracted an estimated 20,000 delegates from over 150 countries. In 2010, the city will welcome the European Gymnastics Championships, bringing with it an injection of spending in excess of €3 million into the local economy. That same year, Marketing Birmingham was vested with an additional responsibility for the attraction of new inward investment to the city, assuming the budget and responsibilities formerly discharged by the Council's Locate in Birmingham organisation.

In Jane Austin's novel *Emma*, the snobbish Mrs Elton says: 'They came from Birmingham, which is not a place to promise much.... One has no great hopes of Birmingham. I always say there is something direful in the sound'. It is now over 30 years since the NEC opened its doors, and as we have documented above much has been achieved since then in a sustained effort to use tourism to revitalise the economy and bridge the so-called 'perception gap' in which dated images and prejudices are at odds with the reality of 21st-century Birmingham. Post-industrial Birmingham is gradually becoming more clearly and accurately etched on to the national and international psyche, and central to this transformation has been the City Council, supported by its two delivery mechanisms – the NEC Group and Marketing Birmingham. Much is still to be done, but the portents are encouraging. Five years after the G8 had been staged in Birmingham, Bill Clinton recalled his time in the city in a piece which appeared in the *Times* newspaper: 'I was astonished ... when I saw how beautiful it (Birmingham) was. The buildings, the art, the use of the water. It is an extraordinary jewel of a city, and one that I think is not very well known outside the United Kingdom. I was bowled over when I was there. It is quite wonderful' (*The Times*, 2 October 2002).

Case Study 4: Gothenburg 1991–2010

Gothenburg & Co has pursued an ambitious event-led tourism strategy over the 1991–2009 period, gaining great confidence from its hosting of the World Athletics Championships in 1995, and latterly staging those for European Athletics (2006) and World Figure Skating (2008). The 2006 European Athletics event is estimated to have attracted a TV audience of nearly 900 million people and brought about a local economic benefit worth €90 million. Gothenburg itself (population 495,000) grew rapidly in the 19th century as a port and industrial centre, and early in the next century what were to become global giants (Volvo and SKF) established themselves in the city, the latter on the back of the invention of the world's first self-aligning ball bearing. The industrial and trading prowess of Sweden's second city was, however, severely eroded towards the end of the last century, and the requirement to diversify the local economy led *inter alia* in 1991 to the formation of Gothenburg & Co.

From the onset, Gothenburg & Co enjoyed the support and financial backing of Gothenburg City and its Mayor. The company's stated vision was to see Gothenburg become '… a preferred choice among cities in Europe by being one of Europe's most pleasant and attractive urban regions to visit, to live and work' (Bjerkne, 2008). Armed with this vision, the organisational concept underpinning Gothenburg & Co. was that it would form a collaborative platform for committed and active partnership across the local public and private sectors to implement a long-term strategy designed to position Gothenburg on the world stage and to maximise tourism revenues. Testimony to the commitment of the partners is best illustrated by reference to company finances. Gothenburg & Co.'s 1991 budgeted income was just €2 million, the lion's share of which came from Gothenburg City Council. By 2008, the company's income had undergone a 15-fold expansion, by which time the municipality's share was just 33% (€10 million), with the remainder comprising trading income (€8 million) and private sector donations and sponsorship (€12 million). The latter derived mainly from upwards of 20 major companies and institutions located in the region, amongst whom were Volvo and SKF; the University of Gothenburg and Chalmers University of Technology; Handelsbanken and Swedbank; and companies such as Nobel Biocare (dental solutions), SKANSKA (construction) and Castellum (real estate).

In line with the budgets, tourism as a component of Gothenburg's economy grew significantly over the 1991–2008 period, with the volume of overnight stay tourism more than trebling (refer Table 2.6 in Chapter 2). In 2008, 3.3 million bednights were recorded, representing an injection of €2.3 billion into the local economy, translating itself into 17,600 FTE jobs. A key external driver of growth during this period was low-cost carriers: in 2001, there were 24 direct flights to the city, of which only one could be described as a low-cost carrier. Six years later, the comparable figures were a total of 53 direct flights, 26 of whom were low-cost carriers. The resultant ease of accessibility enabled Gothenburg & Co. to exploit a mostly already existing infrastructure and superstructure so as to penetrate short-break, conference and event markets. Bordering the city centre to the east are entertainments and events areas: the entertainments quarter comprises *Liseberg* (amusement park), the *Universeum* (science centre) and the *Varldskulturmuseet* (museum of world culture); the events quarter features the *Gothenburg Convention Centre* (see below) and the *Scandinavium* (arena) and the recently redeveloped *Gamla Ullevi* (sports and football stadium). However, the compact and largely pedestrianised *city centre* is Gothenburg's main attraction, with its broad avenues, its trams and canal, its graceful terraces and squares, its old town and harbour, its abundant parkland and its established museums and galleries – notably the *Konstmuseum* (art and photographic gallery), the *Stadsmuseum* with its Swedish East India Company storyline and the *Röhsska Museum* of design and applied arts.

Hotel capacity in Gothenburg is dominated by the 704 room *Gothia Towers* which is situated on the premises of the Gothenburg Convention Centre which has a capacity of 8888 seats spread across 46 rooms. Within a 30-minute walk of the Convention Centre, there are 8600 hotel rooms. Gothenburg & Co.'s short-break marketing campaigns focus on Swedish, Norwegian, Danish, British and German markets, and are promoted by media relations activities, mailings and the web portal *goteborg.com* which receives annually in the region of 1.7 million unique visitors. The main promotions centre on major events, Christmas, and city break offers. The latter – the 'Gothenburg Package' – combines overnight accommodation, breakfast and the 'Gothenburg Pass' – a plastic or electronic card which gives the visitor access to visitor attractions, tours, car parking, public transport, as well as discounts in shops and restaurants.

In 2008, Gothenburg & Co.'s *convention department* was instrumental in bringing 112 conferences to the city region, with an associated delegate expenditure estimated at €39 million. Amongst the prestigious conferences held in Gothenburg during that year were the European Society of Therapeutic Radio Oncology (4500 delegates), the Swedish Society of Medicine (7000 delegates) and the World Editors Forum, the latter event attracting 1800 newspaper owners, chief editors and publishers.

The company's *events department* has a three-pronged role. Firstly, it masterminds bids for 'flagship' sporting and cultural events, and at the time of writing is bidding to host the 2013 World Championships in Athletics. Examples of events which the Department helped to bring to the city have been the Ice Hockey World Championship, the Guldbaggen Film Awards and the Volvo Ocean Race. The range of events sourced and won spans festivals, championships and award ceremonies, through to high-profile football matches (e.g. the 2004 UEFA Cup Final) and concerts by performers such as Paul McCartney and Metallica. Bidding activity of this kind involves close, routine, and at times exacting levels of partnership work with event organisers, venues, environmental health and protective services, media and sponsors, as well as local clubs, associations and other community groupings. Secondly, the company's events department leads on the development and marketing of a citywide festivals calendar, coordinating and working with the city council, the universities and the company's private sector partners. It directly produces some of these events on an annual basis, for example, the summer Gothenburg Party festival and the International Science Festival, while others are delivered as 'one-off' items, for example, the 2005 Housing Exhibition. Thirdly, and more generally, the department provides project management and funding advice and support to municipal, voluntary and private sector event organisers.

Bill Bryson's travel book *Neither Here Nor There* (1991) contained a most unflattering portrait of Sweden's second city. He lampooned the weather, the cost of living, the service, the shops and the food, bemoaning the public drunkenness, and suggesting the authorities there were hell bent on squeezing 'all the pleasure out of life' (Bryson, 1991: 153). It is a picture which today seems unrecognisable. Under the direction of its ebullient and charismatic founder CEO, Claes Bjerkne, Gothenburg & Co came to epitomise purposeful partnership working and private sector leverage, as well as leading edge operational and managerial practices (e.g. mobile city card, the 'Goteborg Package', balanced scorecard assessment). Its role and accomplishments in relation to major events is exemplary. All this was recognised in 2007 when Gothenburg and Co. was the recipient of a richly deserved award from ECM simply entitled *Best European City Tourist Organisation* (Gothenburg & Co., 2010).

Case Study 5: Dublin 1992–2010

Dublin (population 506,000) experienced a dramatic expansion of its economy in the last decade of the 20th century and the first half of the current one, reputedly becoming one of the most prosperous cities in the world. Tourism played an integral part in the emergence of Ireland and its capital as the 'Celtic tiger'. The origins of Dublin's CTO can be traced back to March 1964, when *Dublin Tourism* was formed as part of a national restructuring which created six area tourism organisations in the country (Sugrue, 2006). In its early years, Dublin Tourism played out a fairly low key role, reflecting the fact that up until the late 1980s Irish tourism was marketed essentially in terms of what we have referred to previously as the 'great outdoors'. In the case of Ireland, this translated itself into green and windswept landscapes and friendly country folk. Dublin was emphasised less as a destination in its own right, and more as an access and departure point. By the late 1980s, however, it was becoming recognised locally that tourism could contribute significantly to the rejuvenation of what was a then ailing city economy. In 1988, the Dublin Chamber of Commerce published a report outlining a way forward, and titled it 'Destination Dublin: The development of Dublin's economy through tourism'. In 1992, the Irish Times ran a provocative headline: 'Dublin – failing to make the tourism grade' (McManus, 2001: 103). There was to be a potent response to this critical headline.

Facilitated by greatly improved air and ferry services, overnight tourist trips to Dublin grew by 151% between 1990 and 2007, with nearly all this being attributable to high-spending international visitors (Table 3.3). In 2007, 4.4 million overseas tourists injected €1.4 billion into the Dublin

Table 3.3 Volume and value of overnight stay tourism to Dublin, 1990–2007

	Trips (000's)			*Expenditure (€ millions)*		
	Overseas	*Domestic*	*Total*	*Overseas*	*Domestic*	*Total*
1990	1254	1039	2293	NA	NA	
1995	2134	1209	3343	NA	NA	
2000	3369	912	4281	793	138	931
2005	3937	1232	5169	1282	224	1506
2007	4449	1316	5765	1450	264	1714

Source: Board Failtie (2008)

economy, 85% of all tourism spending in the city. Their visits were spread reasonably evenly across the seasons. The typical international tourist to Dublin came by air (92%), was on holiday (51%), stayed in a hotel (51%), and spent freely – an average (in 2007) of €326 per person per trip (Flanagan & Dunne, 2009). Dublin was attracting nearly two-thirds of all overseas holiday tourism to Ireland, with visitors from mainland Europe having overtaken British tourists as the principal source markets. Moreover, the city was now perceived as trendy and fashionable: its image a heady mix of symbols old and new – harp, the River Liffey, Molly Malone, literary giants, vibrant night life, Guinness, painted doorways, the 'craic' (Irish for a laugh), Riverdance, rugby, U2 and last but not least, the Dubliners them-selves with their trademark friendliness and independence, and their love of words, music and singing. Dublin became a place to party. By 2008, 48% of Dublin holidaymakers were less than 35 years old (Flanagan & Dunne, 2009).

In Dublin, the characteristic double-digit annual tourist growth which characterised the 1990–2007 period was accompanied by sustained – at times almost frenetic – private sector investment in hotels, restaurants, licensed premises, tours and retail. In contrast to the 1970s and 1980s, when hotel capacity had declined as a consequence of the troubled politi-cal situation in Northern Ireland and the availability of cheap holidays in the Mediterranean, new hotel development fuelled by European Union (EU) grants characterised the 'Celtic tiger' of the 1990s. The five years, 1995–2000, witnessed a near doubling of the stock of available rooms. Dublin Tourism at long last flexed its muscles, and began to promote heav-ily to mainstream as well as niche city break markets. An opportunistic niche promotion in the autumn and winter of 1998 lured 8000 high-spend-ing Icelanders to Dublin, principally to avail themselves of the opportuni-ties to shop and to party. They spent an estimated €10.3 million over and above the cost of their airfares and accommodation. Working alongside Dublin City Council, Dublin Tourism also promoted 'one-off' major events, as well as annual festivals such as the *Dublin Theatre Festival* (1957 onwards) and the *International Film Festival* (2003 onwards). Notable 'one-off' events were the official opening of the Tour de France (1988), the Cutty Sark Tall Ships Race (1988), the MTV Europe Music Awards (1999), the Special Olympics (2003), the Beckett Centenary (2006) and the Ryder Cup (2006). Four years in the creation and built at a cost of €38.1 million, the *Guinness Storehouse*, a novel 'brand experience' visitor attraction, opened in December 2000 on the site of the company's St James's Gate Brewery. By 2002, it was attracting 725,000 paid admissions a year, complementing existing landmarks and attractions such as the *General Post Office*, the *James Joyce Centre*, *Trinity College* and its *Book of Kells*, *Dublin Castle*, the *National Museum* and *Kilmainham Gaol*. The latter was restored by volunteer groups in the 1960s, and was attracting 160,000 paid admissions per annum by the year 1999.

On the back of the seemingly never-ending tourist growth, Dublin Tourism – led vigorously by its Chief Executive Frank Magee – adopted a bullish commercial approach, especially to the generation of web and tourist information sales. Its annual report for the year 2006 recorded 300,000 unique visitors to its website and 1.6 million callers at its overtly commercial tourist information centres, and indicated an associated earned income of €3.8 million (Dublin Tourism, 2007) during that year. A thriving commercial membership scheme brought in a further €229,000 of fee income. In 2006, these earned income streams together accounted for 75% of the company's gross income of €5.5 million, with the remaining one-quarter derived from the public purse. In 2008, the company could boast that its city web portal visitdublin.com – in five languages and with over 5000 pages – was the best of its kind in Europe. The web site registered over 4 million unique visitors in that year, averaging out at 340,000 per month, with impressive functionality with respect to online accommodation and car hire bookings, Google mapping, free calling to Ireland (Go2Call) and podcast 'iWalks' (Flanagan & Dunne, 2009).

The economic recession brought a sudden halt to the year-on growth which had characterised Dublin's tourism economy since 1990. In 2007, tourist numbers and revenue remained more or less static, and in the following two years dropped by 2.5% and 9.0%, respectively. Dublin Tourism has responded to these challenges within the framework of its 'Making it Happen' three-year regional tourism plan (Dublin Tourism, 2007). Under the banner of its *'Truly, Madly, Deeply … Dublin'* destination brand, the company is undertaking a range of innovative online marketing campaigns with supporting press and PR activities, claiming impressive results as measured by CTR (click through rates) and other metrics (Johnston, 2009). Sales of the company's Dublin Pass, introduced in 2004, have grown steadily to reach 34,278 in 2008 (Johnston, 2009). From 1 June 2008, the Dublin Convention Bureau – formed in 2003 as a partnership of

Dublin Tourism, the Irish Hotels Federation, the Association of Irish Professional Conference Organisers and Dublin City Council – was absorbed within Dublin Tourism, marking a desire fully to exploit the opportunities soon to be presented by Convention Centre Dublin, currently under construction and set to open in September 2010.

Dublin in the 1970s and 1980s was economically depressed, run down and inward, wearing the scars, financial and physical, of its longstanding, troubled relationships with mainland Britain and Northern Ireland. It uneasily wore the mantle of a capital. Jill and Leon Uris could reflect in 1976 that 'The only world-class boulevard runs but a few blocks. One would be hard pressed to find many of the trappings of grand stature that usually go with a national capital' (Uris & Uris, 1984: 85). Visiting it for the first time in the early 1980s, the author was struck by the low standard of living, the beggars, the uninspired cuisine and the antiquated state of the taxis ferrying visitors to and from the airport. Even today, aspects of Dublin's infrastructure fail to match its capital status, the requirements of its tourism sector and its fashionable image. Although progress is being made, there are still bad roads, poor signage and problems of litter, drunkenness, drug dealing and uncleanliness. A survey of visitors undertaken in 2008 revealed that over one-fifth (21%) felt the city was dirty (Flanagan & Dunne, 2009). That aside, Dublin in the space of two decades has become truly cosmopolitan, offering everything you would expect from a capital city. Visitors now flock to it from all over the world and – as its CTO recognises – its tourist competitors are less Belfast and the cities of the British mainland and more 'Amsterdam, Vienna, Prague, Barcelona and Budapest' (Dublin Tourism, 2007: 11).

Observations and Interpretations

Each of the case studies presented above shows how self-sustaining tourist growth was established against a background externally of improved access and a broadly favourable economic climate, and internally of proactive CTOs/CMAs, supportive city governments and an engaged private sector. In all cases, *political and strategic leadership* emanated from the city government, with strong commitment and ambition evident from the office of the Mayor or Leader of the Council downwards. *Tactical and operational leadership* was secured through purposeful and well-resourced CTOs/CMAs, led by effective and influential chief executive officers. These organisations were able to galvanise on a continuous basis the support and day-to-day involvement of tourism trader interests and other important local organisations and institutions: notably, event, visitor attraction and venue providers; media; universities and colleges; and key players in the local business community. Our case studies exemplify how the dynamics of city tourism development centre on these so-called endogenous local factors and, in particular, the endeavours and activities of the local public and private sectors. Enabled by transport providers, it is cities and their governments, institutions, businesses and people who build and generate their tourism and profile. The roles of the national government and national tourist organisations are, at most, only marginally supportive. Against this broad canvas of locally engendered growth, one can contrast the broadly planned and supply-led tourist superstructural approaches which have characterised Birmingham, Glasgow and Barcelona with the more opportunistic carrier and market-conditioned ones epitomising Gothenburg and Dublin.

A difference between the five cities is evident with respect to image and identity. In terms of their tourism traffic, Dublin and Barcelona are the 'established premier league' whereas Birmingham, Gothenburg and Glasgow are 'up and coming first division'. The fundamental variable here would appear to be city image. Dublin and Barcelona have used tourism to cement a strongly positive image grounded in a clutch of powerful socio-cultural associations which serve to differentiate them from other city destinations. Tellingly, neither city has introduced a formal branding platform such as those we will discuss in Chapters 7 and 8. Despite having made significant progress in cultivating post-industrial identities for themselves, image for Birmingham, Gothenburg and Glasgow remains to this day much more problematic. As we shall see in Chapter 7, all three cities have undertaken city branding projects in an effort to transform their images for the better, but these have met with a patchy level of success. In this way, city image works fundamentally either to enable or constrain, and to separate 'premier' from 'first'.

A fundamental continuity across all five cases is 'needs must'; the sense in which each city was 'hungry' to develop its economy through tourism and create a more favourable image and reputation, and was willing to make a sustained, long-term and ultimately brave commitment to pursue that path. Urban tourism from the vantage point of the 1970s, 1980s and 1990s was an unproven, high-risk path for each of our five cities to follow. Few would have then predicted that our five cities, with their ruptured economies and weak or negative reputations, would by 2010 be known globally and rank as leading European tourism destinations – city tourism's 'new kids on the block'. As we have seen, the CTOs/CMAs reviewed in the five case studies have particular attributes and strengths: Barcelona Tourism is noteworthy for the size and variety of its earned income streams; the Glasgow Marketing Bureau for its conference ambassador scheme and the extensive development of its attractions base; Birmingham for its rejuvenated city centre and its prowess as a meetings destination; Gothenburg & Co. for leading-edge marketing practice and the events it sources, bids for, facilitates, and produces; and Dublin Tourism for its commerciality as evidenced by its TIC and online sales.

Comparing the five CTOs/CMAs, however, one is struck by the similarities: the grounding in local-level public–private partnership; the all-important strategic alliance with the municipal authority; the marketing of a wider city region; the requirement to secure the financial and operational participation of tourism trader interests; the preoccupation with 'high-yield' events, city breaks and meetings markets; the sense in which the 'backbone and lifeblood' of CTO/CMA activities have latterly come to centre on the web and the internet; the commercialisation of web and visitor servicing arrangements; the intimate and many-sided relationship with media; and the shared professional language and culture, despite all the difficulties of cross-cultural communication.

A final observation is that the lessons to be learned from these five case studies are best revealed by reference to elsewhere! In Britain, for instance, Leeds, Sheffield and Bristol are not 'on the map' in the way that Glasgow and Birmingham now are, and in the final analysis that is down to the absence in the former three places of commitments, approaches and processes which are ambitious, purposeful and long-term. In the fiercely comptitive environment of city tourism, as many fail (wholly or in part) as succeed and the critical variable is decisive collaboration of the local public and private sectors. Reflecting on Gothenburg & Co's 18-year campaign, its Chairman recently remarked: 'You may be applauded for what you have achieved, but you win trust by taking bold action' (Gothenburg & Co., 2010: 5).

Part 2

City Tourism Organisation

Chapter 4

City Tourism Organisation: Structure and Operations

Introduction

A survey of city tourism organisation by ECM conducted in 2004 (Dominicus) discovered that on average a CTO/CMA had 47 staff, earned 32% of its income and was labour intensive, spending 78% of its overhead budget on staff. The proportion of income derived from the public purse was as low as 15% for the Bergen Tourist Board, rising to 100% in the case of the municipal department of tourism responsible for promoting the Spanish city of Tarragona. The Vienna Tourist Board (VTB) boasted the largest annual budget, then standing at €16 million, while the smallest was a mere €170,000, belonging to the city council department of tourism in the Czech Republic city of Olomouc.

This chapter examines the structure and operations of city tourism organisation. We begin by looking at how and by whom CTOs and CMAs are governed (the governance) and then at the professional marketers (the executive) who – led by the CEO and reporting to the governance – orchestrate and undertake the marketing, communications and visitor servicing activities. The aim of CTO/CMA marketing and communications is to create new visitors, especially those staying overnight in serviced accommodation forms, while visitor servicing majors on the provision of information, traditionally through the medium of TICs, but increasingly through remote electronic points and mobile communications.

This chapter draws upon case material from mainland Europe, with special but not exclusive reference to the VTB. The Board was established in 1955 under Vienna's Promotion of Tourism Act, and evolved into one of Europe's largest and most successful CTOs. The VTB today has a staffing compliment of 107, 77% of whom are female (Weiss, 2009). Over half (56%) of its 2009 budget of €27 million derived from a tax on local accommodation providers, with the remainder comprising municipal grant (20%) and private sector/earned income (24%). Interestingly, for the first 30 years of its existence, relatively small amounts of funding were derived from the bed tax. A change of VTB President in 1985 saw the previous incumbent, a local

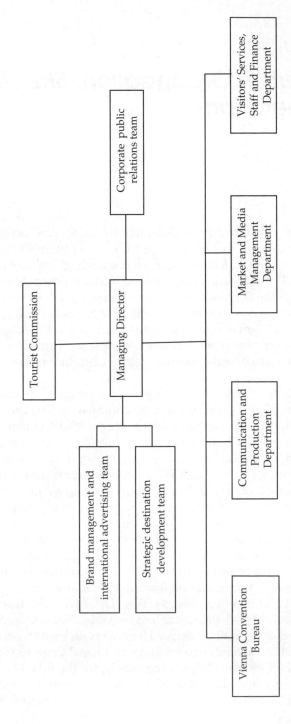

Figure 4.1 Organisation of the Vienna Tourist Board

government politician holding down the cultural portfolio, replaced by the city councillor for finance. The new President changed the basis of computation from a flat rate to one levied as a percentage (2.8%) of the overnight price, significantly boosting bed tax revenues. Moreover, the new, incoming President was also persuaded of the need to invest additional monies in the VTB, drawn from the general budget of the municipality. This was done on an almost year-by-year basis beginning in 1986. The combination of increased bed tax revenues and municipal grant was to furnish the VTB with the handsome budgets on which branding, advertising, media and travel trade activities are currently implemented on an impressive global scale, as we shall see in the section following 'Programmes and Activity Areas'.

As well as being well resourced, VTB's marketing approach is noteworthy for its strategic orientation backed up by robust and extensive market and other intelligence. This is embodied organisationally in the work of VTB's Strategy Group and its *Strategic Destination Development* team (see Figure 4.1). The Board's first corporate plan – the 'Vienna 2010 Tourism Scheme' – contained the aspiration to have by 2010 grown Viennese tourism to 10 million bednights from a base 2002 figure of 7.7 million. The 10 million target was in fact attained in 2008, the year in which work began on the second plan – the 'Vienna Tourism Concept 2015'. In this plan, the goal is to increase bednights by a further 1 million. This represents a 'big ask' inasmuch as 2009 figures indicated 9.8 million bednights in that year, representing a 3.8% year on fall from 2008, reflecting the impact of global recession.

By dint of the VTB and other case materials, the focus of this chapter is on the public–private partnership model of CTOs/CMAs as opposed to local government-centred forms of tourist administration which are to be found in certain cities (see Chapter 1).

Governance and Executive: Vienna Tourist Board, Visit Oslo and Valencia Tourism

The governance of city tourism organisation approves policy and budgets, delegates authority to the executive to formulate and implement policy, monitors operational performance and otherwise ensures that the CTO/CMA trades solvently and legally. The public–private partnership model will typically have for its governance a chairman or president leading a board of senior and influential 'volunteers' – volunteers in the sense that they are usually unpaid and their 'main' jobs will lie elsewhere, either as politicians, local government administrators, industry managers and leaders, business persons, academics and media/communications specialists. At heart, these groupings of amateur 'volunteers' provide what are essentially supervisorial boards.

In the case of the VTB, the board is called the Tourist Commission and it is headed by a President nominated by the municipality – currently Renate Brauner, who is a Vice Mayor of the Vienna city government with a portfolio comprising finance, economic affairs and public utilities. In addition, there are two vice-presidents and 14 other 'ordinary' board members. With the exception of three board members nominated by the chambers of commerce, labour and agriculture, respectively, all the remaining appointments (including that of President) are made by the municipality. As such, these nominations are from the political parties of the State of Vienna on the basis of proportional representation, that is, according to the number of votes obtained by the party at the last municipal elections. Perhaps remarkably, this has never allowed the business of the board to become politicised on a party basis, and all decisions of the board have been consensual and unanimous ones. The majority of board members nominated by the municipality comprise senior-level representatives of the tourist industry – hotels, theatres, restaurants, youth hostels, the airport and so forth. The board meets four times a year.

In contrast, the boards of other CTOs /CMAs are smaller and less biased in favour of municipal nominees. At more or less the other extreme to the VTB, for instance, is the eight strong board of Visit Oslo, all of whom are nominated by the private sector shareholders of the company. As such, the board is currently chaired by a city hotelier whose 'main job' is Managing Director of the Grand Hotel Rica. The remaining board members comprise a director of Scandinavian Airlines, a marketing consultant to the Oslo Concert Hall, the managing director of Tusenfryd theme park, the head of property at Oslo airport, the marketing and communications director of the Norwegian National Opera and Ballet and two more city hoteliers. The board meets five to six times a year to discharge its supervisory duties, and in addition attends the company's annual general assembly of shareholders. Effectively the shareholders are the company's commercial members.

A third example, the governance of Valencia Tourism, is chaired by the City Deputy Mayor who as President heads a Board of Directors comprising the presidents of the local chamber of commerce, the city's trade and exhibition centre and the Valencia Confederation of Employer's Organisations, together with representatives drawn from the 250 companies who are members of the foundation.

Operating Structure: Vienna Tourist Board, Visit Oslo and Valencia Tourism

The day-to-day management of CTOs/CMAs is in the hands of a professional executive led by the CEO – variously titled Chief Executive, Managing Director, Executive Director or Chief Executive Officer. VTB's current Managing Director is Norbert Kettner who has been in post since

September 2007. Prior to this, Kettner had been heading up Departure Ltd – a funding body established by the City of Vienna to assist local designers to gain international recognition for their products. Before that there had been journalism and a period as the local government press officer serving Renate Brauner. The appointment of the Managing Director is by nomination of the Tourist Commission on the President's recommendation.

The executive under Kettner is organised into seven functional teams and departments as shown in Figure 4.1. The three staff teams ('stabsstellen') work closely with the Managing Director and provide services corresponding to corporate public relations, strategy (including market intelligence) and brand communication and international advertising. The four departments shown in Figure 4.1 are the mainstream marketing and communications 'engine rooms' whose activities are designed to win new overnight stay visitors across business and leisure tourism, and to otherwise supply visitors with information and other products and services as summarised later in this chapter.

By way of further illustration, Visit Oslo's operating structure (see Figure 4.2) is led by the Managing Director, Tor Sannerud. The staffing

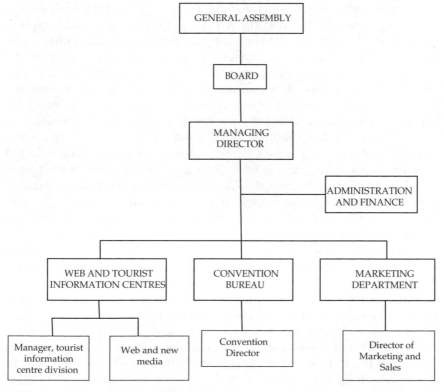

Figure 4.2 Organisation of Visit Oslo

compliment provides for 33 full-time posts, as well as 35–40 seasonal positions to supplement the summer activities of the TIC network. Figure 4.2 indicates that the 33 core staff are deployed across five departments responsible for administration and finance (5), leisure tourism, marketing and media management (9), conventions (3) and web, new media and tourist information centres (16). The senior management team of Visit Oslo effectively brings together the Managing Director and the departmental heads for leisure marketing, conventions, visitor servicing and finance. Its job is to steer the implementation of the annual work programme, while maintaining budgetary control both in terms of ensuring that income targets are being met and costs contained.

Figure 4.3 depicts the operating structure of Valencia Tourism. Here, the staff are organised into five functional departments covering communications, promotions, marketing, research and external relations and visitor servicing, with a support department for finance and administration.

Programmes and Activity Areas

A framework within which to understand CTO/CMO programmes and activity areas is set out in Figure 4.4. Flowing from the organisation's core purpose and mission are two programmes: the first, the image programme, seeks to raise the destination profile, positioning the city in the minds of the key target audiences; the second, the tourism programme area, aims to maximise the net value of tourism to the local city economy by creating new visitors, by effective visitor servicing, and by otherwise enhancing the quality of the visitor experience. The image and tourism programme areas then subdivide into four and five activity areas, respectively. The *image programme* comprises the following activities: brand development and implementation; media management centering on press and PR work and the hosting of press visits; event production and marketing; and corporate citizenship schemes which maximise financial as well as 'off-the-balance sheet' contributions from local companies and city institutions such as the universities. The *tourism programme* majors on leisure tourism and convention marketing activities designed to attract high yield, overnight stay business to the city; the servicing of visitors (primarily through TICs); venue location/finding services to source appropriate meetings and accommodation facilities for event organisers; enhancing the quality of the visitor experience (mainly through accreditation schemes); and the administration of commercial membership schemes – the 'sister' networks to the corporate citizenship schemes mentioned above, but this time aimed at tourist trader interests who for the payment of a fee are afforded priority in terms of exposure and referrals. A final set of activity areas deliver services which support corporate objectives

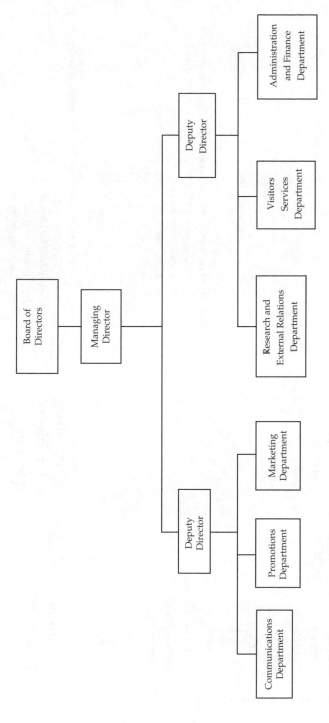

Figure 4.3 Organisation of Valencia Tourism

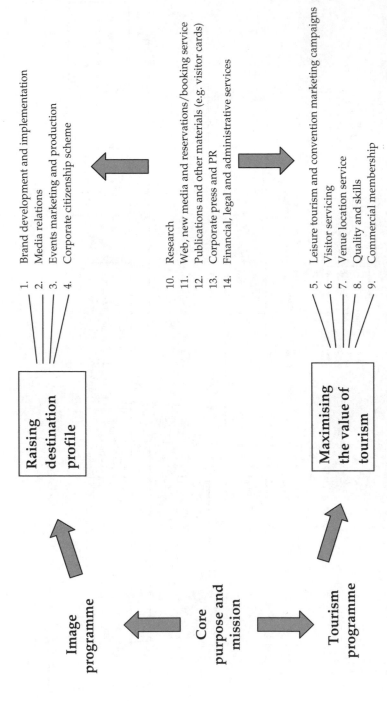

Figure 4.4 Anatomy of city tourism organisation: one core purpose and mission, two programmes and 14 activity areas

(notably finance, legal and administrative services, and corporate press and public relations) as well as the mix of activities contained within the image and tourism programmes, namely research and intelligence, web and new media, publications and other products (e.g. visitor cards).

Of course, individual CTOs/CMAs vary significantly with regard to the extent and nature of their image and tourism programmes (as we know already from the typology presented in Chapter 1) and few will be involved in all 14 activity areas. For instance, the VTB has neither an events marketing and production capacity, nor does it organise corporate citizenship and commercial membership schemes, and its role in relation to quality and skills is slight. The schema in Figure 4.4 is essentially an aid to understanding; it enables the operations of a specific CTO or CMO to be contextualised and conceptualised, as we can now do with specific reference to the marketing activities of the VTB.

Raising Destination Profile, Attracting Business and Leisure Tourists and Visitor Servicing with Special Reference to the Vienna Tourist Board

Vienna does not have a formal, 'umbrella' city brand of the kind discussed in Chapters 7 and 8. The VTB does, however, have a carefully contrived destination brand for the city, and VTB's *Brand Management and International Advertising* team ensures that the brand shapes the organisation's consumer marketing approach, its stakeholder relationships and its corporate identity. Work on developing the current brand with its *Vienna now or never* strapline was initiated in 2008 and launched in October 2009. This followed extensive consumer research on the city's image and reputation undertaken by a Vienna-based public relations company (the Skills Group) working in association with the global communications agency Fleishman Hillard. The new destination brand itself was developed by the advertising agency Jung von Matt/Donau, replacing the 'Vienna waits for you' advertising line developed for the VTB by Young & Rubicam in 2001.

'Vienna now or never' has five sets of 'brand modules', the strongest of which is the city's 'imperial heritage', followed by 'music and culture', 'savoir vivre', 'functionalism' and 'urban quality and ambience'. In terms of practical application, 'Vienna now or never' cleverly seeks to capitalise on the city's strong and positive identity, focusing on heritage as well as more contemporary strengths, conveying the message that somehow or other people are really 'missing out' if they do not commit to visiting Vienna. One advertising image, for example, shows a couple embracing against a Viennese backdrop with the caption: 'At this very moment, a heart is again being stolen in one of the safest cities in Europe – it's a pity that it's not yours.' Another image of the 17 bells tolling at St Stephen's

Cathedral is accompanied by the line: 'Can you hear them too? Oh, you're not even here.'

Within the framework of the destination brand, VTB's *Communication and Production Department* conducts advertising (conventional and online) and manages two web sites: the consumer portal www.vienna.info in 14 different languages and the B2B site for the tourist industry www.B2B.vienna.info. This department also produces an annual publications port-folio which currently contains 230 separate print items (brochures, posters, leaflets and maps) which are translated into 20 languages. Working with industry partners, advertising and sponsorship revenues are maximised. A good example is the Vienna city map. Nearly 4 million are produced each year, half of them distributed free of charge by Global Refund, a hotel delivery service. Paper and printing costs are almost entirely covered by advertising monies derived from approximately 30 companies, with title page advertising courtesy of Manners chocolate wafers. Other advertisers are mainly attractions, restaurants, cafes and shops. It is interesting to note that each year the map takes approximately six months to progress from design to print, and consumes 200 tons of paper; piled up high, the maps would be 60 times taller than St Stephen's Cathedral!

Examples of the 'niche' marketing campaigns currently being under-taken by the VTB are 'Vienna, wine and design' and 'Shop and wine'. In the former campaign, city break holiday opportunities in the 'shoulder' months of October and November are promoted, with Austrians, Germans, Italians and Swiss as the target country markets. Approximately 1.2 million advertising supplements are distributed along with 50,000 bro-chures. In a similar vein, a 'Shop and wine' campaign has been run each year since 2003; it covers the 'low'-season months January–February and the markets are Austrian residents and the countries of Germany, Italy and the United Kingdom.

Finally, the Communication and Production Department are responsi-ble for two other important projects. First, it markets and distributes the Vienna Card; at the time of writing and at a cost of €18.50 to the tourist, the card offers over a four-day period a variety of discounts at more than 200 shops, visitor attractions restaurants and cafes, as well as 'free' public transport for 72 hours. In 2009, 300,000 such cards were sold; nearly all the principal hotels in Vienna act as sales outlets, as do tour operators abroad, travel agencies in Vienna (working as handling agents for tour operators), and the city centre TIC. Secondly, there is the Vienna Experts Club which was formed in 2002 as an outcome of deliberations by VTB's Strategy Group. It provides for a continuous training programme aimed at improv-ing and updating the 'product knowledge' of hotel staff, incoming travel operators and others. The Club currently has more than 600 members.

In support of the above marketing activities, VTB's *Market and Media Management Department* conducts an annual programme of marketing activities targeting media and the travel trade in 20 western European countries, as well as the United States, Japanese and Asian 'source' markets. The Department has over 20 staff split across 'media' and 'market' functions, and it is important to separately consider the work of each.

VTB's *media team* is each year responsible for sourcing and hosting press visits to the city by journalists, photographers and cameramen, and for organising press events outside of Vienna (VTB, 2010). This activity generates copious and highly positive coverage about the destination in newspapers and magazines, and in television, radio and web formats. In a steady and sustained manner, this helps cement Vienna in the public's mind. In 2009, for instance, the media management team helped and looked after over 1000 media representatives from no less than 43 different countries, introducing them to diverse aspects of the city's appeal through individually arranged programmes. In addition, the team was active overseas, organising 47 press briefings and events. As a result, Vienna was the subject of approximately 3000 items of positive media coverage in print and online media. In one travel piece, Britain's *Sunday Express* newspaper referred to Vienna as 'the coolest city for a weekend break', as did the Italian fashion magazine *Glamour* – 'la capitale piu cool del momento'. The journalist Erica Wagner writing in *The Times* advised her British readers to swap Disneyland in favour of the Austrian capital, labelling it as 'the best amusement park in the world'. Other consumer magazines celebrated Vienna as 'music to the ears and stomach' (*Vinni*, Finland), as 'a metropolis for gourmets' (*Tele*, Switzerland) and as 'a sexy mix of history, art and thoroughly modern chic' (*Elle*, Canada). *Cuisine* in Australia carried a feature on Vienna titled 'Waltzing to its own tune' in which journalist Jane Adams 'eats and sips her way through Vienna, a reborn jewel of the Danube'. Likewise, Felicity Carter, writing in Australia's *Delicious* magazine, summed up the city as being as 'famous for its music and architecture as it is for its strudel and schnitzel … an eclectic blend of old and new'. More prosaically, Britain's *OK Travel* entitled a destination report 'Oh Vienna – there's much more to the Austrian capital than you think'. In America, *The New York Times* published print and online pieces on the attractions of Vienna's Neubau district and on leading examples of the city's viticulture, while *The New York* magazine ran a culinary-based review headed 'Skip the Schnitzel in Vienna' (Vienna Tourist Board, 2010).

Television features generated by the media team in 2009 ranged from exposure on RTL 4 in the Netherlands, MDR in Germany, and France 3, through to Hong Kong Cable TV, MTS Maori Television and India's Zoom!TV. For instance, Belgium's Flemish television and radio network VRT carried a report on Vienna focusing on its music past and present, and containing interviews with leading musicians.

It is worth noting that VTB's media team do not convert the coverage into advertising equivalence as is often the case with other CTOs and

CMAs (refer, for instance, to Table 5.1 in Chapter 5 and the case study of Visit York in Chapter 6). Instead, the Board measures success by the volume, focus and content of the media coverage garnered as a consequence of the press visits and events it organises.

VTB's *market team* focuses its activities on trade intermediaries – especially tour operators and travel agencies – and directly on prospective consumers themselves. The team attends each year upwards of 200 trade and consumer shows, workshops and presentations and organises trips to familiarise the travel trade with what the city can offer to tourists – the so-called 'fam' trips as they are known in the business. In this way, approximately 3000 representatives of the travel trade are 'familiarised' by the VTB each year, and as a result incorporate Viennese tourist 'product' into their promotions and packages.

With respect to business tourism, the VTB established a not-for-profit department dedicated to that purpose in 1969 – the *Vienna Convention Bureau*. The 11-strong team work proactively to attract conferences, incentive travel, exhibitions and company meetings to the city, each of which brings delegates and other business visitors, so as to directly benefit conference venues, hotels and professional conference organisers (PCOs). Alongside Paris, Vienna ranks as the world's top city in which to confer internationally, and nowadays business tourism (associated with which is lucrative per capita expenditure) accounts for some 12% of all overnight stays in Vienna. Key to the work of the Bureau is its maintenance of a comprehensive database on prospective international, association and other meetings. This is vital inasmuch as wooing and winning conferences emphasise long lead times, as event organisers plan their events years ahead. For international meetings, this usually follows the practice of meeting in a different continent every year. With the intelligence that a particular event was held, say, in Spain in 2009, this will focus the Bureau on seeking to bring it to Vienna in and around the year 2014. Based on 'hot leads' of this kind, the Bureau works not as a PCO itself, but as a 'one-stop shop' offering free, friendly and professional support to whosoever is the event organiser – be it a PCO or an organising committee or an individual. In this way, the Bureau assists organisers by preparing bids; by sourcing venues/hotels; by hosting inspections and familiarisation trips; and by helping with the delivery of the event proper through the provision of welcome packs, city cards, destination displays and 'giveaway' bags, umbrellas, pens and the like. In this way, for instance, the Bureau helped bring 22,617 delegates to Vienna in 2007 to attend Europe's largest congress – the European Congress of Cardiology.

VTB's *Visitor Services, Staff and Finance Department* includes 20 staff working from a city centre TIC situated behind the Opera House, as well as a separate service centre. The tourist centre is demonstrably consumer focused, opening 365 days a year, 10 hours a day, and receiving some

400,000 visitors per annum. The complimentary service centre processes approximately 200,000 electronic and postal enquiries each year, providing an online accommodation reservation service, and dealing with customer complaints. As its name indicates, this department also administers human and financial resource functions.

The work of the departments, as shown in Figure 4.1 and as described above, represents city marketing on a grand scale!

Observations and Interpretations

As we noted in Chapter 1, CTOs and CMAs come in all shapes and sizes. Amidst their characteristic diversity, however, the schema in Figure 4.4 shows how they are all reducible to a single core purpose and mission, to a structural division into governance and executive, and to a configuration of operational responsibilities spanning either one or two programmes and up to 14 discrete activity areas. The Vienna case study is notable because the CTO there sits on a continuum half way between private sector-led CTOs/CMAs such as Visit Oslo, Berlin Tourism and the Geneva Tourism and Convention Bureau, and local government administered ones such as the Munich Tourist Office, the Bruges Tourism Department and the Culture and Tourism Department of Reykjavik City Council.

The Vienna case also illustrates how budgets reflect the political priority afforded tourism in a city, and how individuals (invariably politicians) play a key role in accessing increased resourcing. Crucially, the structuring of CTOs/CMAs into governance and executive enables city marketing decision making and strategy to be made accountable yet at the same time de-politicised, facilitating managerial autonomy as well as planned and commercial approaches. Even where nominations to the board follow party political lines – as is the case with the VTB – the affairs of the board remain supervisorial and quintessentially apolitical. Fundamentally, this allows a business discipline to obtain and prevents a situation in which the direction and management of the organisation become subject to considerations other than what is 'best for the business'.

Operationally, the VTB works to a formal plan and an explicit destination brand, and takes pains through its corporate public relations work to communicate its role and achievements – hence, the small teams devoted to strategy/intelligence, brand and corporate public relations working closely with the VTB Managing Director. From there, we have the logical flow through to the four mainstream and frontline marketing and visitor servicing departments, focused around what are the key result areas for every CTO/CMA, namely short break and conference marketing and sales, media coverage, travel trade activity designed to persuade agencies and operators to handle and market the available city tourism product, and visitor servicing activities which inform and enrich the tourist's experience and his/her time in the city. The culture and personality of the teams and departments varies across these activity areas, presenting a sizeable corporate set of challenges with respect to communicating and creating a sense of organisational unity and common purpose. In setting up and leading CTOs/CMAs, it is important to embrace these and other challenges, and it is this to which we now turn our attention in the next chapter.

Chapter 5

Setting Up and Leading City Marketing Agencies

Introduction

For 19 years (1990–2009) the author occupied chief executive officer positions in four CMAs. In each case, I set up the organisation 'from scratch', and in each instance the CMA was established to promote a major English city and its wider hinterland. In what follows, I recount my experience in starting up and leading the four CMAs, highlighting eight indispensible 'building blocks', as well as major 'lessons learned' in the form of nine key reflections. The 'building blocks' are first and foremost *funding*; followed by the recruitment of *governance* and *executive*; the provision of *office space, IT infrastructure* and *brand platform*; and, finally, the introduction of *commercial membership* and *corporate citizenship* schemes within which the participation and support of the private sector may be secured. In the author's experience, it takes approximately one and a half years to put in place these 'building blocks' during which time stakeholders are characteristically anxious for 'quick wins' and more or less immediate results: for the CEO, managing these tensions and the others which flow from the interplay of 'letting go' and 'payback' considerations (discussed below) become dominant preoccupations. All too easily, the CMA can become a scapegoat and a repository for all those 'worthy', but unfunded functions that are assiduously avoided by other city agencies. It is important to counter the criticisms and the detractors, and to avoid 'drift' of mission and core purpose. In short, the CEO has to work hard to avoid becoming what I used to refer to as 'head of blame', and he/she must ensure that the organisation sticks to its mission and does not degenerate into a 'catch all'.

Though the evidence base for this chapter is autobiographical and in parts anecdotal, it is nonetheless reliable in that it is based upon reports, press cuttings and notebooks. I have endeavoured to avoid the account of my 19 years degenerating into trivia and valediction, or worse still into self-aggrandisement or self-justification. I have striven to be balanced and objective, emphasising shortcomings as well as successes. There is no academic literature known to the author pertaining to the establishment and leadership of city tourism organisation. As such, this chapter will hopefully comprise a useful as well as interesting starting point.

Sheffield (1990–1996) and Destination Sheffield

On the afternoon of 4 January 1990, I was interviewed for the post of Director of Tourism, City of Sheffield. I was then a senior lecturer in tourism at Strathclyde University. I had been there some 13 years, teaching and researching about tourism, and now I wanted to 'do it'. Prior to interview, I had been assessed by a recruitment specialist and his candidate profile of me (unwittingly circulated to me) included the unflattering observation that 'he is not someone who is immediately warm (he does not smile very much) and I wondered at first if he was an academic rather than a practical marketer'. Notwithstanding this, the phone rang later on in the evening, and I had got the job.

At interview I had emphasised that I saw the number one priority as being the establishment of a CMA to promote Sheffield on the back of ambitious investments which were then being made in sports stadia, shopping and culture, as a prelude to the city hosting the 1991 World Student Games. The person who telephoned me that night was one Norman Adsetts, a local businessman who had founded the Sheffield Insulations Group plc. He was an enthusiastic, charming and well-connected 'Mr Sheffield'-type figure, who amongst many other roles occupied the chairmanship of Sheffield Partnerships Ltd – a body recently established to promote a positive image of the city and under whose aegis the new tourism and image initiative was to take shape. Mr Adsetts advised me that the interview panel had been unanimous and then, with what seemed to me a disconcerting degree of honesty, he declared that the panel 'didn't really know what they were looking for'. However, he went on to say my local roots were important. As a born and bred Sheffielder, 'you're one of us' he said.

As the city's first ever Director of Tourism and an employee of Sheffield Partnerships Ltd, I reported in my first year directly to Norman Adsetts. So *reflection number 1* in city tourism is that the local political bosses, senior officials and leading businessmen do not necessarily know what they want from either the tourism and image programmes or from the CEO they are hiring! Your job as CEO is to articulate for them the 'game plan' and the tactics; to embed both the agenda and the strategy for city marketing. This resonates with the central thesis of Erik Braun's book on city marketing (2008), namely city marketing succeeds to the extent that it is embedded in city governance – in its strategies, in its institutions, and in the mindsets of its politicians, public officials and business leaders.

I started work as Director of Tourism for the city of Sheffield on Friday 15 June 1990 and – reflecting the fact that my employers 'didn't really know what they were looking for' – I was, in my first year, little more than a title and a briefcase. My 'office' turned out to be a desk in the corner of a windowless open-plan office housing the city's inward investment agency (the Sheffield Development Office) which, in turn, was part of the City Council's Department of Employment and Economic Development (DEED). It soon became apparent that the tourism/city image ambitions of this department were modest and also 'controlling' inasmuch as DEED sought to 'monitor and guide' my work as Director of Tourism through a 'steering group' comprising middle-ranking council officers drawn mainly from DEED!

A key departmental project of DEED was to develop a visitor attraction devoted to popular music in a part of the city designated as an embryonic cultural industries quarter. In principle, such a project was to be welcomed as a way of capitalising on the city's fledgling Red Tape recording studio and its musical heritage (Joe Cocker, Human League, Def Leppard, etc.) while at the same time putting the city 'on the map'. Unfortunately, the business plan for the proposed centre for popular music was deficient in several respects which led me to doubt its commercial viability. Crucially, I felt the location and the esoteric nature of the exhibitory being designed would combine to produce a visitor attraction with only limited market appeal. Insufficient provision was also being made both for parking and post-launch marketing. Throughout my six years in the Sheffield job I was placed in the unenviable position of having publicly to be supportive of this project, especially to media and to public sector grant regimes (including the National Lottery), while privately using every opportunity to raise my concerns. It is sufficient to say DEED was unhappy with my behaviour. (When the €17 million National Centre for Popular Music eventually did open its doors in March 1999, by which time I had moved to Coventry, all my worst fears were realised; the Centre received only a handful of visitors and closed just over one year later to become a live music venue and latterly the student union building for Sheffield Hallam University.)

Alongside my misgivings about the Centre and the steering committee set up to guide and monitor my work, it soon became clear that DEED were unsympathetic towards my key short-term objective which was to set up and head an independent CMA to market the city. To turn that concept into reality, I therefore avoided my office and the steering group as much as possible, and got 'out and about', 'networking' myself throughout the summer and autumn of 1990. I did a lot of listening and talking, as I explained my CMA concept to business people, politicians, council officials and media, seeking finance as well as moral endorsement and support. Such was the continued antipathy of the Employment and Economic Development Department to my CMA 'cause' that I was eventually obliged early in 1991 to turn to the Leader of the City Council and seek his help in resolving matters. Although he came down on my side, there was a bruising aftermath in which my relationships with DEED went from bad to worse.

Bit by bit during 1991 – there was no official, single moment of creation – an independent public–private partnership was established: a tripartite coming together of Sheffield City Council, Sheffield Development Corporation and local hotels and meetings venues. It was called *Destination Sheffield* – a straight copy from the Destination Stockholm referred to in Chapter 1. Such partnerships were rare in those days; so this was pioneering both as a new breed of local tourism administration and in the sense of the local public and private sectors working together. To that end, the City Council was 'letting go' of what had formerly been its responsibility, as overseen by a tourism subcommittee of councillors chaired by a senior politician, Peter Horton, and then discharged by a low-ranking council tourism officer.

In August 1991, Destination Sheffield moved into office space at Leader House – a fine but somewhat dilapidated Georgian property in the heart of the city centre – and it was there that the first meeting of Destination Sheffield's board of directors was held on 3 September 1991. The legal status of Destination Sheffield was that it was a company limited by guarantee and it was registered as such at Companies House. The board of directors was chaired by Don Lyon, Group Chief Executive of H Turner and Sons Ltd – a regional chain of newspaper and sportswear outlets. I quickly warmed to this dynamic and shrewd local businessman who was to be my 'boss' for the next four and a half years. Always positive, constructive and to the point, Don said that he was looking to learn something about tourism from me. In return, he would help me to become a businessman – to 'walk the talk' of my title as Managing Director of Destination Sheffield.

The governance of Destination Sheffield comprised a 12-strong board of directors chaired by Don Lyon, as well as three advisory committees – called panels – for image, events and tourism, each of which was chaired by a board member. The panels were introduced at Don's behest, and were afforded the role of monitoring the implementation of the company's image and tourism programme areas, enabling the board proper to concentrate on being 'custodian' of strategy and with otherwise ensuring that the company traded solvently and legally. This arrangement worked well, and through the panels there was the unanticipated advantage of giving individuals and organisations opportunities to become involved in Destination Sheffield – opportunities that otherwise they would have been denied. 'Better to have them in the tent', as Don Lyon would say (or words to that effect!). In every city to which I subsequently went, I would trot out panels for image, events and tourism – save in Nottingham where my strenuous efforts to carve out a significant events role for the CMA encountered frustrating 'letting go' and funding obstacles, and ultimately came to nothing.

In practice, the board of directors of Destination Sheffield left strategy and day-to-day management to the Managing Director, acting as a challenging yet essentially supportive framework within which I would present on the company's immediate past performance and future proposed activities. The board was private sector led, inasmuch as it was chaired by a businessman and there were just two local authority nominees (one of whom was the Deputy Leader of Sheffield City Council), with the remainder drawn from the tourist trade, the wider business community, the universities, media, the Sheffield Training and Enterprise Council and the Sheffield Development Corporation. Most board members were 'passive' in the sense that they did little other than attend the monthly board meetings. My day-to-day contacts on the board were with Don Lyon and two of the other, more committed board members; the Sheffield Development Corporation's Director of Finance and the Director of Facilities at Sheffield Hallam University. Although he was not a board member himself, Councillor Horton was my main link to Sheffield City Council.

In terms of funding, Destination Sheffield was financed by Sheffield City Council, the local tourist trade, and the Sheffield Development Corporation. The latter was a 'fixed-term' body established and grant aided by the national government to regenerate the former steel and metal manufacturing heartland of the city, known as the Lower Don Valley. Each leg of the three-legged stool put in some pump-priming cash, with the lion's share in that first year – €271,000 (76%) – deriving from a City Council core funding grant. On the back of this, the company sought to 'lever' other sources of funding, notably private sector contributions, trading income and 'external' grants (i.e. non-local authority grant income). In this way, by 1996/1997 Destination Sheffield's annual income had increased substantially, standing at €783,000 and supporting a staff of 16. By that financial year, only 29% of company income was now attributable to the City Council core funding grant, whose value in gross terms had in fact been reduced by €50,000 to a 1996/1997 figure of €221,000. The remainder, the non-local authority 'levered' income, came from external grant regimes (35%) and 'earned' income streams (36%). The latter comprised a cocktail of monies drawn from tourist information sales, accommodation commissions, and fees and sponsorship deals with the private sector. The former – the external grant income – started to come on stream in significant amounts from 1995, following a successful application for €283,000 of European Regional Development Fund (ERDF) assistance spread over a three-year period, 1995/1996 to 1997/1998. The grant was formally approved on 11 April 1995 at a meeting in Barnsley Town Hall, despite opposition from a seemingly unlikely quarter – the Yorkshire and Humberside Tourist Board. I suspect that this was not entirely unrelated to the fact that Sheffield City Council had on my advice withdrawn from membership of the Yorkshire and Humberside Board, on the grounds that the €20,000 annual subscription fee was better spent directly by Destination Sheffield. At any rate, by the 1996/1997 financial year, the City Council

core funding grant of €221,000 was now 'levering' €562,000 of other financial contributions – a leverage ratio of €1.0 : €2.5, and in Council circles this
strengthened my hand against detractors such as DEED, giving the author
a reputation for being able to make 'something out of nothing'.

Alongside successful leverage, however, came the requirement to trade
solvently and this became a perennial struggle. Indeed, the author learned
during his Sheffield years that there was an inherent and chronic vulnerability in a financial regime reliant on earned income, fixed-term external
grants and a city council subvention which could all too easily be reduced
or withdrawn completely. (Tourism spending by local authorities in the
United Kingdom is in statute terms an area of discretion and is therefore
one which is always ripe for cutting.) This vulnerability first came to a
head with Destination Sheffield in the summer of 1995. The cost of a
redundancy deal consequent upon an internal restructuring exercise carried out in that year, combined with a reduction in Sheffield City Council
core funding, obliged me to identify midway through the 1995/1996 financial year €53,000 of cost reductions. These ranged from closure of a TIC at
Sheffield's railway station, built by donations assembled from the private
sector, through to the sale of my company car. Such were the sacrifices
that had to be made to ensure Destination Sheffield remained a 'going
concern'.

On a wider financial canvas, Destination Sheffield acquainted me for
the first time with the interplay of 'letting go' and 'payback' considerations. The participation of stakeholders in company activities, and their
financial commitments in particular, was premised on *'letting go'* so as to
permit managerial independence of operation and the full exploitation of
levered income streams. 'Letting go', however, carried with it the *quid pro
quo* of *payback*. The latter was the implicit and sometimes explicit desire on
the part of stakeholders to influence the scope and content of Destination
Sheffield policies and programmes, and to gain commercially or otherwise from company operations. Tourist trader interests sought to realise
commercial gains, while public and other interests (e.g. the local authorities, larger companies and educational institutions) looked to returns in
the form of wider community gains – notably support for their 'pet' projects (such as the National Centre for Popular Music), enhanced profile for
themselves and the city and increased local income and employment.
Resolving or at least managing the tensions between 'letting go' and 'payback' fell squarely on the shoulders of the Managing Director, assisted at
board level by the Chairman. The interplay of 'letting go' and 'payback' –
inimical bedfellows – shaped the workings of Destination Sheffield, and
all the other CMAs I was subsequently to set up and lead.

So it is that destination marketing organisations in England finance and
indeed structure their existence. *Reflection number 2*, borne of my Sheffield
experience, is therefore that powerful as the public–private partnership

'model' is, it is accompanied by financial vulnerability and inherent tensions. To reiterate, the 'mix' of local authority, earned and external grant income is an unstable one. Local authorities frequently exercise their discretionary powers to make cuts to core funding, while funding from external grant regimes is typically won on a competitive basis and is for finite periods of time, with the regimes themselves 'coming and going' in line with the changing priorities of new political regimes. Earned income levels are conditioned by the state of the economy. The extent to which city tourism organisation is in accounting parlance a 'going concern' is therefore nearly always an issue and a worry for CTOs and CMAs. As exemplified above by my experiences at Sheffield, it becomes a moot point whether or not the CTO/CMA is able financially to sustain itself over the medium to long term. Formidable skills in assembling and earning funding are prerequisites for initial and continuing viability, as are reconciling the tensions between 'letting go' and 'payback'. In this respect, the CTOs/CMAs record of leverage will be a significant variable shaping stakeholder perceptions of the extent to which the organisation is succeeding or not.

I resigned from the Sheffield job at the end of July 1996, shortly after 'Sheffield Plays at Home' – a cultural festival organised and marketed by Destination Sheffield to coincide with the Euro' 96 football championships. All of the festival's €127,000 funding had been raised externally, with core sponsorship of €44,000 from the supermarket chain Morrisons. Euro '96 as a soccer tournament brought 66,000 visitors to the city from Denmark, Portugal, Croatia and Turkey, and they injected some €6.5 million into the local economy as they spent money in hotels, restaurants, pubs and shops. The Danes literally drank the city dry! By the summer of 1996, Destination Sheffield's event-led tourism strategy was seen to be beginning to work. It involved close collaboration with the Major Events Unit of Sheffield City Council in respect of event bidding and hosting arrangements for major sporting championships. It also meant *inter alia* delivery of sometimes exacting accommodation booking requirements. Without computerised reservation systems, the company's file, card and fax-based venue location service struggled manfully (but in the end more or less successfully) to handle the complex accommodation bookings requirements entailed by major events such as the 1993 European Swimming Championships, the 1995 Special Olympics and the 1996 World Masters Swimming Championships.

To capitalise on the city's rich industrial history, Destination Sheffield had introduced innovative visitor trails, factory tourism visits, heritage plaques and Walkman tours, as well as weekend breaks featuring real ale pubs and the city's burgeoning night life. It had done much to persuade the City Council, the universities and metal manufacturing companies to store and catalogue a heterogeneous collection of 'made-in-Sheffield' tools and cutlery, latterly in 2010 becoming a permanent gallery – the Hawley

Collection at the Kelham Island Industrial Museum. 'Destination Showcase' was the banner under which the company sought to win conference business, and it had secured some lucrative successes, notably the annual conference of the National Federation of Retail Newsagents over a five-year period from June 1997. In 1996, the company's commercial membership scheme – Business through Tourism – recruited Sheffield Theatres as its 100th fee paying member.

By the summer of 1996, there was a feeling that the city was 'turning the corner' and that Destination Sheffield had played a visible and creditable part at the start of the city's post-industrial regeneration. My six years at Sheffield had been classic 'learning by doing' and while I was conscious of mistakes I had made, especially human relations ones, the local papers reported on my resignation by opining that I had done a good job, almost embarrassingly so with lines like:

- 'John Heeley has made Sheffield tourism a reality. Now it needs to be nurtured and expanded.'
- 'Vital work John started must go on …. His quiet methods of persuasion often harvest fruit from seemingly barren trees.'

Garnering comments such as the above-demonstrated another essential leadership ability which was to persuade local media to 'take up and talk up' the city marketing agenda and strategy. The comments above also alluded to my 'quiet' leadership style – something which would come into sharp relief seven years later in Birmingham. As a postscript to my Sheffield years, the financial fragility of Destination Sheffield to which attention was drawn above led in November 2000 to my successor as Managing Director being made redundant, and the company being wound up and its assets transferred to Sheffield City Council. This sad and drastic course of action was necessitated against a backdrop of forecast trading deficits of €62,000 and €84,000 for the 2000/2001 and 2001/2002 years, respectively.

Coventry (1997–2000) and Coventry and Warwickshire Promotions

In August 1996 I stood in the ruins of Coventry Cathedral for a photo-call to introduce the man 'poached' from Sheffield to 'do the business' for Coventry. I took up office at Coventry on 2 January 1997, and four months later *Coventry and Warwickshire Promotions* (CWP) was launched as an arms-length company with the help of 'privatised' monies from Coventry City Council. In its first year, CWP had a budget of €445,000, all of which came from the City Council, and included the wages of five 'inherited' council employees – the rump of the Council's former tourism team. Morale and activity levels within the team were at a very low level, with just one publication and no strategy, leverage and research discernible. Four years on, CWP had 28 full-time staff and a 13-strong board of directors, supported by advisory panels for tourism, image and events. CWP's annual income had reached €2.5 million by the year 2001/2002, with just 40% now coming from the City Council; the rest a mixture of external grants and earned income sources. Once again, there was success on the leverage front. Indeed, Coventry City Council had stepped up its funding to enable CWP to produce and market a cultural events programme whose annual centrepieces were the Godiva Procession and Festival (June), the Coventry Jazz Festival (August) and various Christmas festivities.

By 2001/2002, CWP was pitching hard across corporate communications, business and leisure tourism marketing, visitor servicing and event production and marketing. Thanks largely to a supportive Director of City Development, I had been (unlike at Sheffield and Birmingham and Nottingham to follow) afforded a 'top table' position by the City Council in respect of planning and development, and on behalf of CWP I was contributing significantly to major urban regeneration schemes as well as more routine, but equally important infrastructural matters such as signage, public art, street cleanliness and the like. In 1999/2000, the company had also taken 3000 'frontline' staff through a novel Coventry Welcomes You with Pride training scheme which majored on customer handling, product knowledge and pro-active 'selling on' of the city's advantages.

One of the biggest successes at Coventry was the festivals programme – badged *Spirit of Coventry* and produced and marketed by the 'in-house' events team at CWP. Through this team, the company delivered overtly populist cultural programming which was innovative, bold and controversial, making it difficult for stakeholders to stick to the 'letting go' principle. The most striking example was Coventry's Millennium Eve celebrations which featured a French tightrope walker making his way across a thin steel rope suspended between the spires of Holy Trinity Church and the old cathedral. This spectacle attracted huge global publicity and was rapturously received by residents, cementing CWP's reputation and position. However, when the Head of Cultural Events at CWP had first suggested the idea of the tightrope walk, there was opposition from both the City Council and the clergy – mainly out of an overly cautious fear that the tightrope walker would fall to his death on the night. In the end, I went to the press in order to overcome opposition from councillors and clerics and *vox populi* went with me. There was a real sense, therefore, in which CWP as an organisation 'walked the line' on that Millennium Eve. Failure would have made us an orphan, but success on the night meant that there were a thousand fathers, including some of the very clerics and councillors who had been steadfast in their opposition. One councillor was even willing to acknowledge her mistake. The Chairman of the

City Council's Arts and Culture Policy Team went on record as saying that she had been 'guilty of a serious lack of vision'.

While CWP had 'walked the wire' to universal applause, there were two important projects during the author's tenure at Coventry which were less than successful, with attendant lessons learned. First, there was city branding. As we shall see in Chapter 7, by the late 1990s the idea was gaining currency that cities ought to brand themselves in the way that, say, supermarkets, banks and motor car manufacturers did for their products and services. Glasgow with its 'Mr Happy' logo and its 'miles better' tagline had come to be seen as a role model. In Coventry there was scant resourcing available for city branding, and for me there was little experience upon which to call. The political will to 'do a Glasgow' was there, however, and it fell on the shoulders of CWP to orchestrate a city branding initiative. Utilising the services of a local design agency working *pro bono*, CWP rolled out a *Coventry inspires* logo and strapline in May 1999. Despite an effective, poignant launch using school children, followed by some early enthusiasm and bannering, this branding project was never applied systematically – like so many city brands before and doubtless many more to come. The reasons for the high failure rate evident amongst city brands are discussed at length in Chapter 7, but for the moment suffice to say that the author's experience at Coventry is well captured by Whitfield (2008) in the following quote:

> DMO … managers and directors often have enviable skills for satisfying diverse agendas but lack experience or the real authority to champion a cutting edge brand concept through the political maelstrom. All too often this results in a *me-too*, watered-down, committee-designed brand proposition that fails to differentiate and squanders resources. (Whitfield, 2008)

This is precisely what happened in Coventry, and the simple lesson I learned – *reflection number 3* – is that 'muddling through' must not be an option in respect of city branding. Effective city branding hinges on the CEO having a clear idea of how to originate a city brand, how to launch it, how to secure post-launch application and how to fund it, all of which we highlight in Chapter 7.

The second 'know what you are doing' lesson from Coventry centred upon *destination management systems* (DMSs). The latter are basically the IT infrastructure used by CTOs/CMAs to collect, store, manipulate and distribute information in all its forms, and to undertake associated transactional activities, notably online bookings and reservations. They came into existence in the late 1990s as a mechanism to avoid what the Americans were then referring to as 'disintermediarisation' – the process whereby intermediaries such as CTOs/CMAs were to be 'killed off' by the web and internet revolutions, as customers inexorably connected themselves to places and venues direct rather than through a third-party intermediary. In 2000, I had attended the annual congress of the International Association of Convention and Visitor Bureaux in Minneapolis, and discovered while I was there that North American CTOs were running scared at the prospect of their imminent 'disintermediarisation' and were introducing DMSs apace.

Returning to Coventry from Minneapolis, I became a zealous disciple of DMSs – first at Coventry, and then at Birmingham and Nottingham. I began to refer to the DMS as the 'backbone and lifeblood' of a 21st century destination marketing organisation. In each of these cities, large amounts of European funding were assembled to provide the financial wherewithal with which to build a DMS – for the installation and running of these systems does not come cheap. The Coventry DMS project, for instance, was made possible on the back of a European Regional Development Fund grant worth €305,000. The project was much delayed and upon completion failed to deliver in terms of the anticipated functionality and the expected commercial returns. With hindsight, a number of classic errors had been made. The scope and content of the DMS specification was insufficiently tailored to the business needs of CWP and to the various end users, namely tourists, media, stakeholders and members. We were insufficiently clear about what we wanted to put in place and about what to do with it when it was in place. Frankly, as CEO I did not at that time understand enough about the new internet and web technologies. A particular weakness was a failure to relate the DMS to the wider landscape of web-based marketing infrastructure, maximising interoperability and links to third-party booking agencies such as Lastminute.com and Expedia. Last but by no means least, income from the project had been exaggerated and the costs understated. I learned from these DMS mistakes; so I fared significantly better second and third times around at Birmingham and Nottingham, but it would have been good at Coventry had we been able to learn from someone else's experience and mistakes. When you are pioneering the leading edge, then leading can often translate itself into a 'bleeding' edge of innovation and experiment. *Reflection number 4*, therefore, is that muddling through must also not be an option in respect of your DMS. Obey the above-mentioned imperatives!

The disappointments at Coventry were, however, outweighed by the successes. In recognition of what I had achieved, I was even afforded a civic dinner on 25 July 2001; a proud and humbling moment, taking place a few days before I headed just 20 or so miles 'up the road' to England's second city. The *Birmingham Post* referred to my having 'worked wonders for Coventry', while Coventry's local newspaper ran an editorial headed 'The man who put Coventry on tourist map .... Through his work Dr Heeley has shown the outside world that Coventry has something to shout about; just as importantly, he has won over many inside the city to the cause'. Embedding the 'cause' – the city marketing agenda – in both Sheffield and in Coventry had been difficult, and I trusted that experience would put me in good stead to do well once again in what was a bigger, more complex and ultimately change-resistant context – what I had referred to at interview as the 'Birmingham bear pit'. I had gone on to say that my days there would be much more than a 'ceremonial rain dance'.

Birmingham (2001–2003) and Marketing Birmingham

I took up office in Birmingham early in August 2001, and left – amidst some debate and controversy – just over two years later. In those two years, a comprehensive reorganisation of city marketing took place, in which three hitherto separate organisations were amalgamated to form a new entity called *Marketing Birmingham*. As we saw in Chapter 3, the three organisations were the BCVB, the BMP, and the Tourism Team of the Economic Development Department of Birmingham City Council. The company name was the easy part; taking a leaf from Manchester and Marketing Manchester, out popped Marketing Birmingham! The rest was not because there was internal and external resistance to the concept of turning 'three into one' and to a radical change agenda designed to ensure that the new organisation would be a fit for purpose, 21st century CMA. Indeed, at interview for the job, the Director of the Economic Development Department of Birmingham City Council had made it clear that in his opinion the City Council should 'lead' on tourism. So, Birmingham from the start was never going to be easy.

On my first day at work in Birmingham, I introduced myself to the receptionist at the BMP and asked her why there was a weed growing on the doorstep leading into the company's Waterloo Street offices. Was that appropriate, I asked, for the organisation that was the guardian angel of Birmingham's image and its tourism? She removed it immediately, and that became my first act as the incoming 'new broom' and it symbolised what was to follow. By the end of my second day, there had been meetings with staff at three different locations, corresponding to the offices of BMP, BCVB and the Tourism Team of Birmingham City Council. All in all, that was just over 100 staff, to whom the message was of an agenda of change, repeating the line that this would be more than a 'ceremonial rain dance'.

Over the following three weeks, an audit of existing activities was completed for the board of directors. With the expiry of European Regional Development Funding into the next 2002/2003 financial year, BMP/BCVB was no longer a 'going concern'. There was a lack of clarity as to core purpose and mission, and there was no strategy, business plan, targets and KPIs. A staff questionnaire indicated morale was low. Information technology was antiquated, and accommodation reservation services were not computerised. Office space was of a poor quality, especially in the TICs. Out of a current year budget of €2.4 million, only €295,000 was being spent on marketing. There was overdependence on City Council funding, and (as has been mentioned already) the Council had recently established its own Tourism Team as a part of the Department of Economic Development – a recipe for duplication, conflict and unfocussed delivery.

The audit report was the backdrop against which a 'way forward' was negotiated with individual board members and, in particular, with the Leader of Birmingham City Council and its Director of Economic Development. The comprehensive restructuring of the way Birmingham promoted itself – the three becoming one to form Marketing Birmingham – was outlined in a paper prepared for the BMP/BCVB board of directors in October 2001. The paper was duly approved, and it was encouraging to have made such good progress in the space of just three months. However, the projects and proposals contained in the paper needed funding. Europe was a vital source of cash with which to equip the new body with the head office, IT and TIC infrastructure needed to promote effectively on the national and world stages. To that end, a substantial €3.3 million ERDF application was lodged at the Government Office for the West Midlands early in 2002.

The new Marketing Birmingham organisation was formally incorporated on 24 April 2002, and in the following September formal approval was given to the €3.3 million ERDF award. With that award, the directors sanctioned the signing of a lease for 8000 sq. ft of prestigious new office space set within the city's new, flagship complex called Millennium Point. Hot on the heels of this, Marketing Birmingham was officially launched at Millennium Point, marked by the publication of a brochure titled 'Our big vision' setting out the new company's core purpose and mission. Just before Christmas 2002, all of the staff from the hitherto three separate offices moved into their new Millennium Point workplace.

Events moved apace in the New Year. On a bitterly cold morning in February 2003, the launch of the Championing Birmingham corporate citizenship project took place in Centenary Square, with one of the founder 'champs' showing his commitment by abseiling down an adjacent city centre tower block to unveil a 45-m-long banner promoting the scheme. How the scheme played out so successfully despite a sceptical board of directors is outlined below. A 'sister' scheme to Championing Birmingham was launched on April 2003 in the form of a commercial membership scheme targeting tourism trader interests. Two months later, there was the opening of what were to become award winning TICs at the Rotunda and in Birmingham New Street. The centrality, quality and welcome afforded to visitors at these centres had at that time no equal in the country, and were the realisation of an aspiration to create 'tourist information centres of the 21st century'. This phrase was designed to convey a quantum leap from the 20th-century time warp in which UK TIC provision and management were then trapped.

A remaining important building block was put in place early in July 2003. Over 1000 school children assembled at the Aston Villa football stadium to celebrate the launch of the *'Birmingham b'* place brand. This was the first ever city brand in Britain to attempt to go beyond the simple slogan and logo-led marketing campaigns which had previously obtained (see Chapter 7) and there were great hopes for it. Writing in the *Birmingham Post*, I spoke of the new 'b' brand affording the city a 'real opportunity to create a sense of place … and a powerful framework within which to market to key audiences regionally, nationally, and internationally'.

Marketing Birmingham had become in just two years the best-resourced and most-integrated destination marketing organisation in England. Its annual budget for the forthcoming 2004/2005 year was set at over €7 million, a part of which was provided by the pioneering corporate citizenship scheme – *Championing Birmingham* whose launch we referred to above. In its first year, this scheme attracted €670,000 of private sector and regional development agency funding. The three universities became 'champs' and so too did Aston Villa football club, property companies, law firms and accountants, as well as world-class brands such as Jaguar and Cadbury Schweppes. A delegation came from Leeds to see how we had succeeded in engaging these sorts of companies and institutions – the 'corporates', as I referred to them – in the promotion of the city. Championing Leeds followed in due course.

I had come across the model for Championing Birmingham thanks to the ECM network mentioned in Chapter 1, and a visit early in 2002 to the offices of Gothenburg & Co. I learned from its Chief Executive Officer how successful his company had been in capturing the involvement and financial commitment of local companies and other institutions. I recruited to the scheme personally, beginning in January 2003, and by July 40 'champs' had contracted to the scheme, donating annually a sum of money of their choice of between €6000 and €17,000. When account was taken of 'money match' assistance from the regional development agency, Advantage West Midlands, this represented a first-year sum of €670,000. So, *reflection number 5* is that fulsome engagement of corporates in the work of a CTO/CMA is possible through the introduction of corporate citizenship schemes in which donations are made in return for networking opportunities and media and other exposures. A lesson from Gothenburg was that it was critically important to 'tell the world who the champs are' and why they are such wonderful corporate citizens. Despite all these successes, however, there was in Birmingham personal criticism from certain individuals and quarters. These comments were far from being representative and came in the main from disgruntled elements of Birmingham's professional services community. After a so-called 'whispering campaign', criticisms surfaced publicly in the wake of my resignation from the post of Chief Executive of Marketing Birmingham in July 2003. They amounted to a view that (a) Marketing Birmingham had sought to promote the city as a tourism destination at the expense of marketing it as a commercial and professional centre and (b) that as its CEO I had too low key a persona, that is I was not a sufficiently powerful and visible 'Mr Birmingham'-type of figure. The criticisms are exemplified in the statements below selected from some of the reportage in the *Birmingham Post*:

- 'where can Birmingham find a "big hitter" capable of battling effectively for this city on a world stage?' Editorial.
- 'We do not want an overt self-publicist and neither do we want a shrinking violet.' Leader of the Conservative Group, Birmingham City Council.
- 'The business world is very disillusioned. There is a feeling of huge disappointment with Marketing Birmingham .... The business community is looking for a visible, credible face and figurehead who can be taken seriously at a national level .... The reality is that Marketing Birmingham should be about vision and visibility, not new computer systems'. Chairman, South Birmingham College.
- 'Birmingham needs a credible individual and Marketing Birmingham seems the obvious home for that person ... Dr Heeley came to personify the problem that Birmingham has. He was chief executive of Marketing Birmingham but he didn't want to lead.' Birmingham lawyer.

Marketing Birmingham had never had a remit to promote the city as a commercial and professional centre; so this criticism seemed really wide of the mark. Indeed, such promotion was specifically the role of another organisation called Birmingham Forward. Spirited defences of my achievements and clarifications of my role were made by the company Chairman, the Chief Executive of the Birmingham Chamber of Commerce and the Leader of Birmingham City Council. The latter went on record as saying that I had over the past two years 'almost single-handedly turned around the ineffective organisation' that I had inherited. In retrospect, the harsh learning point here is that any outsider coming to a city to occupy such a high-profile role needs to ingratiate himself or herself into its 'inner circle'. In this respect, what the Sheffield media had referred to as my 'quiet' ways of getting things done may well have jarred with my detractors and aggravated matters still further. From all of this, I therefore draw the reflection – *reflection number 6* – that to avoid damaging and undermining undercurrents of opinion such as these, then it is necessary to access the 'inner circle' and clearly establish in people's minds the distinction between political leadership of the city – of the Boris Johnson/Mayor Giuliani kind

– and the strategic managerial leadership style appropriate to the professional CEO of a CTO/CMA.

The above publicity and debate made for a somewhat uncomfortable
exit from Birmingham. It also served to obscure the real reasons for leav-
ing the city: the 'push' factor was an inconsistent and often less than supportive board of directors; the 'pull' factor was being 'head-hunted' by
Nottingham and being offered a very handsome salary. So it was with
push and pull that I left Birmingham at the end of September 2003 to start
up number four in the regional capital of the East Midlands; or as a
Midlands business magazine headline succinctly put it – 'Birmingham's
image maker defects to Nottingham!' In the same piece, Nottingham City
Council's Executive Member for Culture, Community Services and
Tourism suggested my appointment marked a step change: 'We want to
take Nottingham on to a European stage', the councillor said. The challenge was an energising one; the problem turned out to be the brand platform introduced to position the city on that European stage and a legend
by the name of Robin Hood.

Nottingham (2003–2009) and Experience Nottinghamshire

Work in Nottingham commenced early in October 2003, and my title
was Chief Executive of Experience Nottingham – or EN as everybody
soon began to call it. The name of the company was something I did not
like, but I was advised this was 'non-negotiable'. EN, as such, was just six-
months old, having been incorporated in May 2003. As a company limited
by guarantee, EN was effectively a 'bolting together' of two unsuccessful
experiments in arms-length partnership working known as Profile
Nottingham and Conference Nottingham. There were six staff and a board
of directors drawn from the two previous organisations, as well as dreary,
dysfunctional office space tucked away in an obscure part of the city's
Lace Market district. On 22 October, in an address to the 'good and great'
of the city, I set out an agenda of change, drawing on all the experience I
could muster from my days at Sheffield, Coventry and Birmingham. There
was a commitment to grow budgets from their present 'pin money' levels,
and to that end plunder the available grant regimes and establish
commercial membership and corporate citizenship schemes. To maximise
the value of tourism locally and to position the city as a leading European
destination, it would be necessary to restructure and revamp the inherited
staff and governance structures. Important 'building blocks' were a city
region brand, state-of-the-art internet-based systems, and a 'flagship' TIC.
All of this would put in place a 'really first class marketing infrastructure',
so that EN could 'walk the talk' of a CMA that was 'second to none'.
I committed to launching a revamped EN early in 2004, and to the
subsequent implementation of a comprehensive and purposeful five-year

strategy which would see Nottingham city and the wider Nottinghamshire county at long last 'punching its weight' on the European stage. Joining forces in this way would eradicate the 'ineffectiveness, duplication and fragmentation' which had so far obtained.

The launch event took place on 30 March 2004 at the Trent Bridge home of Nottinghamshire Cricket Club. Plans were unveiled for the establishment of *Experience Nottinghamshire*, billing it as a new and focused delivery mechanism designed to 'co-ordinate all destination marketing activity previously undertaken by district, county and city organisations'. We were able at this event to report on €674,000 of new monies already secured from grant regimes, the regional development agency and East Midlands Airport. This included €134,000 set aside for the development of a brand identity for the city and wider county area. At the launch, I alluded to the failure of the previous brand which had been introduced by the old Profile Nottingham organisation in 1998. This had featured a Robin Hood logo and an 'our style is legendary' strapline. I stressed the need to introduce a more inclusive, relevant and modern visual identity than one based on Robin Hood alone. My comments were reported in the press the following day, and the debate about the branding platform commenced forthwith.

Legally, Experience Nottinghamshire came into being just over a month later on 3 May 2004. Effectively, the new company was a three-legged partnership of the local authorities, the private sector and the regional development agency – the East Midlands Development Agency. From a base year-one income of €553,000, annual budgets rose in successive years (by what should now be a familiar pattern to the reader) to stand at just over €2.5 million in 2006/2007. The 14 months which followed incorporation in May 2004 saw all the 'building blocks' put in place.

A robust governance of over 60 'volunteers' was established under the leadership of a new chairman, John Saunders. Assisted by the Chief Executive of Nottingham City Council, I had succeeded in recruiting John to the role of company chairman, and he started his two-day-a-month appointment in August 2004. His main job was Chief Executive Global of Experian, an information and credit checking business which had a strong local presence, employing over 2000 people at its various Nottingham offices. Indeed, his stature locally was such that we had few problems persuading able and talented individuals to strengthen the board of directors I had inherited, as well as to 'people' the new advisory panels for image and tourism that were being established.

John Saunders clarified the terms of reference of the governance and presided over its smooth operation, establishing a finance and general purposes subcommittee (chaired by himself) to act as the 'eyes and ears' of the board in between board meetings – an arrangement which worked extremely well. He also played an important part in introducing performance review arrangements as we shall see shortly. As far as the professional executive of Experience Nottinghamshire was concerned, we recruited more or less continuously throughout the May 2004–June 2005 period, in tandem with whatever new monies became available from successful grant applications and from the exploitation of earned income sources. EN by June 2005 had become a 23-strong executive team led by myself.

The first major milestone over the period May 2004–June 2005 was the launch of the company's commercial membership scheme titled Nottinghamshire Tourism on 15 September 2004, referred to in more detail below. The following month was marked by Experience Nottinghamshire's first successful targeted conference bid, when the 2006 annual meeting of the British Association of Sexual Health and HIV was secured for Nottingham, with an anticipated delegate spend in the region of €165,000. In the last quarter of 2004, the company moved into modern, functional open-plan offices, piloted event welcoming activities at the British Open Squash Championships and assembled contributions totalling €75,000 from retailers, entertainment and transport operators to mount a 'generic' Christmas 2004 marketing campaign. This involved inter alia promoting the city and county's Christmas leisure and retailing offer through bus and radio advertising – locally, as well as in the neighbouring cities of Leicester, Derby, Lincoln and Sheffield.

In January 2005 and after over a year's research, consultation and creative development, the board of Experience Nottinghamshire and its Image and Branding Panel approved – unanimously and with great enthusiasm – a new place brand for the city and county whose logo was an 'N'. Great care had been taken to ensure the political leaders of the constituent local authorities of Nottinghamshire – the county and the city council and no less than seven district councils – were 'comfortable' with the 'N' logo. Ironically, in terms of what subsequently was to transpire, the Leader of the Nottingham City Council had rejected earlier logos created by the design agency EN had appointed, and it was only with the 'N' logo sketches that we managed to get him 'onside'. Similarly ironic was the active and enthusiastic part played by the Chief Executive of Nottingham City Council and the Managing Director of the *Nottingham Evening Post* in the deliberations of the Image and Branding Panel under whose auspices the '*Nottingham N*' place brand had been painstakingly originated, refined and finalised throughout the course of 2004. The formal launch of the new brand was scheduled for early March 2005.

On 27 January 2005, another launch event took place, this time for Championing Notts, against a backdrop of the city having acquired over the past two years a horrendous, media-fuelled reputation for murder and for city centre binge drinking and disorder. Indeed, the rationale for Championing Notts was premised on the requirement of the city's principal companies and institutions to join forces to combat 'head on' the negative imagery and damaged city reputation. The means to this end was to vigorously 'project the positives', using the soon-to-be-launched place brand platform. The first year target of recruiting 20 Championing Notts supporters with associated donations amounting to €120,000 was met within just four months. March 2005 milestones were the place brand launch and the linked publication of a countywide publications portfolio showcasing the destination's accommodation stock and its venues and attractions. A €1.2 million DMS went live in May 2005, from which in the following month Experience Nottinghamshire sent out its first 'e-blasts' and recorded its first online short-break bookings. Also in that month, the company's flagship Nottingham Tourism Centre opened its doors, and with that all the 'building blocks' were now in place and Experience Nottinghamshire could go into full delivery mode.

Returning to *Nottinghamshire Tourism*, the simple point is that in tourism, commercial membership schemes are so difficult to get right. The first member recruited to the Nottinghamshire Tourism scheme was an award-winning bed and breakfast operation located in the north of the county, and its 2004/2005 fee was €150. As such, Nottinghamshire Tourism engaged tourism traders – the accommodation providers, event venues, visitor attractions, shops and restaurants – as opposed to the 'corporates' recruited to the Championing Notts scheme. Each and every 'signed-up' Nottinghamshire Tourism member paid an annual fee proportionate to size, and on that basis he/she was expected to receive a commercial return from the resultant business referrals and promotional exposure as EN showcased his/her business on the company's website and in its publications and marketing campaigns. Any commercial operator declining to be a member rendered himself 'invisible' as far as EN's marketing and visitor servicing activities were concerned. Unsurprisingly, tourism trader interests in general have an ambivalent attitude towards paying membership fees: they feel in some cases that they are being 'bribed' into becoming a member; if they do not pay, there is the fear of missing out commercially if their business is not promoted; if they do pay, there is the worry that the exposure they receive will not translate itself into a 'bottom line' return and that the money represented by the membership fee could have been better spent elsewhere. From the perspective of CTOs/CMAs, commercial membership schemes become a 'rod on the back', in that your activities are subject to close scrutiny and can never secure enough 'payback' to individual members, especially in times of economic recession.

Having pointed out the problematic nature of commercial membership, such schemes provide a valuable income stream and an indispensible mechanism with which to galvanise and 'fast track' the involvement of tourism businesses in CTO/CMA activities. In reality, such schemes are a prime organisational 'health check', in that a CTO/CMA which is retaining existing commercial members and recruiting new ones is almost certainly one which is purposeful, relevant and performing well. From a base of 30 members in 2004, Nottinghamshire Tourism grew in successive years, so that by 2009 we could celebrate with great pride the recruitment of our 300th Nottinghamshire Tourism member, and the attainment in that year of €140,000 of member fees. Compared to all the other commercial membership schemes with which I have been associated – in Sheffield, Coventry and Birmingham – this was the one that worked best, partly because we had a highly effective occupant of the post of Membership Coordinator. *Reflection number 7* is that effective engagement of tourism trader interests in the CTO/CMA centres on commercial membership schemes in which fees are paid by businesses in return for marketing exposure and other benefits which will impact favourably on their 'bottom lines'. The trick, of course, is to make sure members do in fact reap those commercial gains!

The low point of my period in Nottingham was a failure to win hearts and minds over the *'Nottingham N'* place brand platform. Despite now knowing what to do, producing a brand platform much admired by marketing professionals, and securing abundant pre-launch 'buy in', it proved difficult and then impossible to implement the brand and maximise adoption and alignment. Effectively, the chances of medium to long-term success were compromised because the editor of the local paper (the *Nottingham Evening Post*) railed against the brand from the launch onwards, on the grounds that Robin Hood should have been the logo and Experience Nottinghamshire ought to have known better. It mattered little to the editor that extensive local 'buy in' had been assiduously assembled (including the Managing Director of the newspaper), that previous attempts to utilise Robin Hood as the basis for a place brand had failed, and that the *'Nottingham N'* was flexible enough to permit Robin Hood-based promotions. His campaign against the brand was marked on the day of the launch with a banner front page headline and supporting editorial calling for the binning of the 'slanty N', as he pejoratively referred to the logo. It was to be the first of several such headlines and editorials, the last of which appeared in November 2008, reporting upon the decision of Nottingham City Council to discontinue using the *'Nottingham N'* and to replace it with a Robin Hood-based alternative. *The Evening Post* headline read: 'The end – Robin returns as city ditches £120,000 slanty N branding'. Whitfield's maelstrom exemplified.

The highpoint of my tenure at EN was the transformation effected in respect of the *Nottingham Tourism Centre*, located on Smithy Row and formerly known as the City Information Centre. The Leader of Nottingham City Council had agreed to 'let go' of the City Information Centre – occupying prime civic/retail space with a commercial rental value of €200,000 – on the understanding that EN provided 'something our residents will be proud of'. Experience Nottinghamshire took over the running of the Centre from Nottingham City Council on a peppercorn rent in June 2005, following a €300,000 redesign and refurbishment, made possible by grant funding secured from the regional development agency. The 'look and feel' of the new Nottingham Tourism Centre, its pioneering 'meet and greet' approach to welcoming visitors, and the range and quality of its merchandising and reservation services constituted a most impressive transformation. After three years of operation, gross annual profit margin had tripled to reach €200,000, a top national award had been won and there had been frequent study visits from TIC managers elsewhere – from Blackpool and York through to Amsterdam and Helsinki. Successful, 21st century TICs, *reflection number 8*, are ones which are big (front of house and back), are located in prime civic/public space, and are run as a business, with a 'meet and greet' approach to callers.

A final observation from my period at Nottingham is about key KPIs. As discussed in Chapter 2, it is fair to say that up until five or so years ago, CTOs/CMAs were 'woolly' organisations, with performance monitoring ranging from fitful to non-existent. The Chairman at Experience Nottinghamshire, John Saunders, said as much to me when he started his four-year tenure in August 2004. There was not much that he did not know about performance management and under his guidance we developed a comprehensive system of monthly reporting against 15 KPIs as set out in Table 5.1. Each KPI embodied SMART criteria – specific, measurable, attainable, realistic and 'trackable' – and were supplemented by the monitoring studies described in Chapter 2, namely industry-wide returns measuring the local economic significance of tourism and campaign-based evaluation studies computing rates of return on marketing investment.

As commented upon in Chapter 2, performance management frameworks such as this represent a quantum leap for the better in terms of accountability and the spending of public and private sector monies. The final reflection, *reflection number 9* is how accountable as opposed to 'woolly' CTOs/CMAs can now be – provided that meaningful KPIs are put in place, alongside the supplementary monitoring mechanisms to which reference has been made.

I left the Nottingham job on 24 June 2009, and once again the local newspaper got it about right. There was praise for my efforts over the past six years, saying that I had 'brought a professional approach to the marketing of the city and the county', pointing to a sustained increase in tourism turnover across city and county since 2003 (refer Table 2.7, Chapter 2), and to the abundant and professional 'packaging' of the destination for events, short breaks and conferences which now obtained. However, it opined that my departure had been hastened by Nottingham City Council's decision to abandon the 'slanty N' and its own campaign directed at 'binning' it, all of which had 'undermined' my position. This clearly had made my position untenable, and so early in January 2009 I

Table 5.1 KPIs: Experience Nottinghamshire 2008/2009

	Percent achievement of KPI as at November 2008
Average number of visits per month to visitnotts.com website	91
Advertising equivalence from media visits	85
Partner income	91
Commission income – conference and short breaks	171
Targeted bids for meetings	90
Bookings value of bids secured	405
Publications income – visitor guides	85
Membership fee income	84
Quality accreditations and training assists	126
Quality and skills – income generation	98
Nottingham Tourism Centre – gross profit margin	90
Nottingham Tourism Centre – average spend per head	165
Championing Notts donations	80
Christmas 2008 – partner income contributions	113
Events sponsorship target	80
Average achievement across the 15 KPIs	124

Source: Experience Nottinghamshire (2008)

had tendered my resignation, and six months later my 19-year career as a city marketing CEO came to an end.

Conclusions

In summary and as exemplified above, the 'start up' and leadership of CMOs/CMAs requires seven strategic/managerial/financial/attitudinal capabilities:

- Experience and knowledge of city tourism organisation, including the IT paradigm which is now the medium through which it conducts its marketing and communications activities.
- A vision of what needs to be done, and the confidence to seek its realisation.

- An ability to raise funding continuously.
- The stamina and social skills to network effectively, including accessing what we have referred to as the city's 'inner circle'.
- Presentational and communication skills.
- Persistence and patience.
- Effective management of human and financial resources.

Arguably, in setting up from scratch a CTO/CMO, these capabilities as set out above are in descending order of significance. For the subsequent consolidation and ongoing development of the organisation, these capabilities are arguably in ascending order of significance. Using these capabilities, the leadership tactics to employ are as follows:

- Provide the CTO/CMA with a clear core purpose, mission and strategy – embed the city marketing/tourism agenda, get local media 'onside', vigorously counter detractors, avoid mission and core purpose 'drift' and resist becoming a 'head of blame' and/or a 'catch all' type of organisation.
- Be adept at managing the inherent tensions within the public–private partnership model, especially as these relate to 'letting go' and 'payback'.
- Develop a prowess for revenue generation, bleeding the grant regimes, and introducing corporate donor and membership schemes and TICs of the 21st century.
- Do not allow city marketing to become confused with city leadership.
- Be performance led through ROI assessments, volume and value returns and SMART-based KPIs.
- Know what you are doing, particularly with DMS and city branding projects.
- In 'starting up' the CTO/CMA, put in place all eight 'building blocks' in the right order.

Throughout, of course, it is important to enjoy the job.

Looking back over 19 years of start ups and leadership, five practical imperatives really stand out for me. First, in recruiting the staff who will spearhead successful delivery, attitude is as important as their professional capabilities. Secondly, it is vital to put in place first-class financial support services to provide timely and reliable management information as well as appropriate procedures and systems. Thirdly, the stature of the board chairman and his/her relationship with the CEO can 'make or break' a CTO/CMA. Especially important here is the role of the chairman in helping at board level to manage the tensions between stakeholder 'payback' and 'letting go', so as to afford the CEO the maximum amount of managerial autonomy. Fourthly, it is important to be brave enough to undertake formal evaluation of the marketing campaigns designed to create new visitors which are the essence of the CTO/CMA role. So often this is the bullet which goes unbitten. Finally, the CEO should 'retain passion and lose emotion', as consistent adherence to this maxim goes a long way to ensure successful start up and leadership.

Chapter 6

York, United Kingdom

Introduction

York (population 193,000) is in tourism terms an urban heritage destination; one of those places which have major historical associations, buildings and monuments; distinctive places of character which have retained some of their best old architecture and other special points of interest. Castles, cathedrals, museums and galleries, birthplaces of the famous, ancient universities, as well as fine streets and squares make them tourist cities par excellence. In England, there are eight principal heritage cities – Cambridge, Canterbury, Windsor, Chester, Oxford, Norwich, Bath and York – and the latter is arguably pre-eminent. An early 20th-century guide to the city eulogised York as the 'realisation of history' itself, and H.V. Morton's *In Search of England* first published in 1927 went so far as to say that the city was 'too good to be true .... York is the lovely queen – as London is the powerful king – of English cities' (Morton, 1939: 207). Seven years later, J.B. Priestley's classic *Journey through England* depicted the city as 'the guide-bookman's paradise, and not without good reason, for if you want the past, here it is, weighing tons' (Priestley, 2009: 294). Towards the end of the century, however, the 1994 edition of *England: The Rough Guide* hinted at another side to the city. While acknowledging that York was the 'north's most compelling city' and that 'no trip to this part of the country is complete without a visit to York', it nonetheless suggested 'a provincial air hangs over the city, and – in summer at least – the feeling that York has been turned into a heritage site for the benefit of tourists' (p. 534). As we shall suggest later, the adjective 'provincial' and the phrase 'turned into a heritage site' encapsulates the crossroads at which York and its CTO currently stands.

The economic upside of 'provincial' York being 'turned into a heritage site' is palpable, and is most clearly evident in respect of the jobs and therefore well-being which flows from tourist spending. Until the late 20th century, confectionery – through household names such as Rowntree's and Terry's – and railway-related industries (notably the regional headquarters of the Great North Eastern Railway and railway carriage and wagon manufacture and repair) had been the staple local industries. At its height, the confectionery industry alone accounted for nearly one-third of local employment, with Rowntrees having over 10,000 employees. The progressive shrinking of the workforces of Rowntrees and Terry's consequent upon takeover by Nestlé and Kraft in 1988 and 1993, respectively means that nowadays confectionery provides only around 2000 jobs in the city. Indeed, between 1984 and 2004 manufacturing employment in York fell by a massive 65% (from 19,500 to 6800 jobs). Tourism, on the other hand, is currently worth in the region of €415 million a year to the city, representing 10,646 FTEs and approximately one out of every 10 jobs locally (Table 6.1). Employment in the hotel and catering sector expanded by 44% between 1995 and 2005, creating 1892 new jobs in this sector alone.

The downside comes as the host community experiences economic, social and environmental disbenefits attendant upon this so-called 'provincial' city being 'turned into a heritage site'. There are two main dimensions to these disbenefits. First, they are concentrated in time and space. As with other English urban heritage destinations, York is predominantly a summer season draw. Spatially, it is also a 'draw within a draw' in that visitors make a beeline for the city's medieval 'core', and in particular the impressively intact *city walls* complete with portcullis gates, an innovative *York Castle Museum*, the *Shambles* – one of the best preserved and most atmospheric olde worlde streets in Europe – and the cathedral. The latter – known as the *Minster* – is the largest Gothic cathedral in Northern Europe, and annually attracts nearly half a million visitors (see Table 6.2). Secondly, the economic benefit of the typical day visiting tourist is relatively low. Visitors to urban heritage destinations in the United Kingdom have a fairly uniform profile from one city to the next, and York is no exception. Its visitors are biased towards older age groupings and the higher professional and managerial strata. Overseas tourists form a significant proportion of visitors (15% in the case of York), but crucially day visitors predominate (86%). The day visitor on average does not stay long

Table 6.1 Volume and value of York tourism 1971–2007

	Number of staying tourists	*Number of day visitors*	*Number of staying and day visitors (million)*	*Expenditure of staying and day visitors (€ million)*	*Employment in tourism (FTE jobs)*
1971	225,000	1,100,000	1.3	–	–
1985	–	–	3.0	–	–
1996	539,000	3,445,000	4.0	283	–
2000	538,000	3,463,000	4.0	285	8555
2007	516,000	3,582,000	4.1	415	10,646

Source: English Tourist Board (1971) and remainder Visit York (2010)

Table 6.2 Admissions to visitor attractions in York 2005–2009

	York Minster	Castle Museum	Jorvik Viking Centre	York Dungeon	National Railway Museum
2005	537,000	184,000	343,000	122,000	760,000
2006	536,000	246,000	352,000	127,000	895,000
2007	461,000	249,000	352,000	134,000	745,000
2008	451,000	269,000	365,000	131,000	750,000
2009	448,000	284,000	347,000	138,000	722,000
Grand total	2,433,000	1,232,000	1,759,000	652,000	3,872,000
Five year average	486,600	246,400	351,800	130,400	774,000

Source: Visit York (2010)

and spends relatively little. In York, day visitors spend on average £54 per visit, compared to €353 for staying visitors.

The concentration in time and space of a predominantly day excursionist-based tourist influx to York – as summarised above – has somewhat inevitably led to the host community expressing ambivalent views towards tourism. This has manifested itself in a variety of ways: from a vacillating stance on the part of the local authority towards tourism through to debates about the value of tourism in the local press. Notwithstanding this, the antipathy of local residents should not be exaggerated. What evidence there is indicates that residents understand the inevitability of tourism to the city, and are mindful, too, of the economic gains. An annual survey of residents undertaken by York City Council indicates that 92% appreciate the economic benefits tourism brings to the city, and only 3% judge these to be outweighed by disbenefits in terms of crowding and pollution. As for the tourists themselves, they keep a coming!

Profile of York Tourism

York's growth as a city tourism destination over the past 60 years has been striking. Using accommodation stock as an indicator, it can be seen from Table 6.3 that since 1950 a near 10-fold expansion has occurred. Initially, growth was stimulated by increased post-war affluence and leisure, greater mobility and a wider appreciation of conservation and history. By 1971 (refer to Table 6.1), it was estimated that 225,000 tourists stayed overnight in the city, with a further 1.1 million visiting on day trips (English Tourist Board, 1972). Over the next 15 years, the attractions base

Table 6.3 Tourist bedspaces in York 1950–2006

	Number of bedspaces
1950	1300
1983	3801
1988	5848
1999	10,854
2006	12,514

Source: Visit York (2010)

of the city underwent significant expansion. The *National Railway Museum* opened in 1975, and quickly established itself as a shrine for lovers of steam locomotion and as the city's most popular attraction. In the space of just six months after its opening, half a million people had visited, with admission levels subsequently bottoming out at approximately three-quarters of a million a year (see Table 6.2). In 1984, the *Jorvik Viking Centre* opened (see below), followed by the *York Dungeon* two years later; a wax-works display with a storyline of murder, torture, execution and punish-ment; as its publicity says, it brings 'York's horrible past to life'!

The Jorvik Viking Centre proved spectacularly successful. Located within a shopping centre, it cleverly capitalised on the archaeological remains of a Viking settlement which had been uncovered as a result of archaeological excavations carried out between 1976 and 1981 by the York Archaeological Trust. A member of the Trust, an entrepreneur and philan-thropist, the late Ian Skipper, was the inspiration behind a visitor attrac-tion concept based on the 'digs'. This started with a 'journey through time' and ended up with a reconstruction of a Viking village complete with ani-mated displays. Skipper also negotiated a funding package for what must then have been a high-risk venture, and devised an arrangement under which the Centre was owned by the York Archaeological Trust and man-aged by a specially formed commercial arm – Heritage Projects Ltd.

When the Jorvik Viking Centre eventually opened in April 1984, even Skipper himself must have been surprised by its rampant success. The early years witnessed frequent and often heavy queuing, with annual admissions numbering approximately 900,000, made possible because the time taken to complete the journey was a mere 12.5 minutes. Trading profits quickly paid off the loan used to finance the development of the attraction, and those earned subsequently were then ploughed back into rescue archaeology projects and the regular refurbishment and refashion-ing of the attraction. The latest such 'refurb', costing €1.2 million, saw the Centre reopen its doors on 13 February 2010 to coincide with the annual week-long York Viking Festival.

As Table 6.2 shows, these three new attractions – the National Railway Museum, the Jorvik Centre and the York Dungeon – together provide for roughly one and a quarter million admissions a year, and their combined effect over the 1975–1985 period was to attract new visitors to the city and extend average length of stay – a classic example of visitor attraction-led tourist growth. By 1985, visitors to York were in fact more than double what they had been in 1971, standing at around 3 million (see Table 6.1). A final spurt of tourist growth saw numbers reach the 4 million mark by 1996; a level at which they appear to have more or less stabilised (refer to Table 6.1).

The rapid and continuous growth of tourism during the post-war era – alongside the preponderance of day excursionists and the sheer concentration of tourists in the compact medieval core to which previous mention has been made – induced some residents to view tourism as a nuisance and a problem. Such sentiments surfaced publicly in 1976 in a series of articles published in the local newspaper, the *Yorkshire Evening Press*. There were references to York residents starting to 'wilt' under the impact of tourism and of the associated pressure on public services. Indeed, the Chairman of the City Council's Recreation and Amenities Committee was quoted as saying that York has 'come very near to choking point'. It is against a backdrop of sustained tourist growth accompanied by a 'tourism: blessing or blight?' debate that we can contextualise CTO operations in York, and it is to the story of Visit York and its predecessors that we now turn.

Origins and Evolution of Visit York

Back in 1969, York City Council had established a *Department of Tourism* headed by a senior local government officer – the Director of Tourism. This followed a protracted period of lobbying by a group of businessmen who believed that tourism ought to be a thriving industry in the city. The Department introduced an approach to attracting tourists based on marketing the so-called 'shoulder' months either side of the main summer season. By the early 1980s, the Council's Director of Tourism was supported by 15 fellow local government officers, eight of whom were seasonal, part-time TIC staff. By this time, however, the attitude of the City Council towards tourism was hardening to one of containment – reflecting concerns about the escalating volume of tourism and the attendant social and environmental disbenefits, as well as the allegedly poor terms and conditions of employment associated with the tourist industry. The then Labour-run City Council was moved late in 1985 to produce a tourism policy statement which *inter alia* referred to

- The need to create 'job opportunities of a quality equal to that achieved in other sectors of the local economy'.

- The 'unusually pervasive "external" effects that this particular industry has on the lives of local residents, and on the viability of other industries operating in the relevant parts of the City'.
- The requirement to strike an 'acceptable balance … between the costs and benefits of tourism'.

The emergent Council policy was therefore one of containment as opposed to proactive promotion of the city as a tourism destination. As a consequence, the Department of Tourism was more or less dismantled, provoking local controversy and even parliamentary debate. In its turn, the City Council's disengagement from tourism provoked a new private sector-led initiative – the *York Visitor and Conference Bureau*. The Bureau was established on 22 July 1987, and its founder chairman was a businessman and local worthy, the late Donald Shepherd – a man whose chief claim to fame lay in his invention of the Portakabin. Denied the succour of local authority financial support, the York Bureau was backed financially by local tourism trader interests as well as by prominent businesses such as Portakabin, Terry's and Rowntree's. In 1990, the Bureau's entire income, €224,000, was derived from private sources.

The York Visitor and Conference Bureau became meaningfully connected once more with the City Council from the mid-1990s onwards, reflecting another shift in attitude on the part of the Council. This was much influenced by what was now an increasingly problematic local economy, as the confectionery industry in particular began to rapidly shed jobs. A 1994 report commissioned by the City Council from the management consultants Touche Ross drew attention to the economic value of York's tourist industry, and the need for local authority and tourist businesses to work together. The *First Stop York* partnership emerged in 1995 as a concrete outcome of the report. As a result, capitalising on the city's environment, and improving the quality of the tourist offer now became the twin priorities – a remarkable change of direction when comparison is made with the policy adopted 10 years earlier. Run by a strategy group chaired by the chief economic development officer of the City Council, the First Stop York partnership provided a framework within which new monies from the local authority and other public sector agencies could be channelled into a variety of tourism-related projects – ranging from award schemes to celebrate employee excellence, through to skills training and the development of an events calendar, as well as attendance at trade shows, marketing campaigns, research and the introduction of 'Residents First' weekends. The latter promotion enabled local residents to avail themselves of visitor attractions free of charge, and was designed to help the host community to identify more positively with the industry. Held each year in January, this weekend promotion currently results in over 20,000 visits being made by the residents of York. The delivery mechanism for these and other projects was invariably the York Visitor and Conference Bureau – now renamed the *York Tourism Bureau*. From 2000, the Bureau also undertook to run the City Council's TIC on behalf of the local authority.

A further rationalisation of destination marketing responsibilities was recommended in the final report of the Future York Group published in 2007; a report once again commissioned by York City Council and this time prepared by a group of prominent and committed local business leaders, with the backing of Yorkshire Forward – the national government-funded regional development agency. The report called on York City Council to 'strengthen its tourism partnerships, by having a single tour-ism partnership organisation, working with the private sector to deliver growth in tourism spend which exceeds Yorkshire Forward's 5% per annum target for the city'. The reference to the regional development agency and its support of the report was significant, in that Yorkshire Forward was potentially a major new source of funding and the mecha-nism whereby a more purposeful regional approach could be pursued, within which York would function as a tourism gateway to the wider region. In the event, 2008 saw the winding up of the York Tourism Bureau and the First Stop York partnership, and their replacement by *Visit York*. As an independent company, Visit York was to be a tripartite partnership of York City Council, local tourism businesses and the regional tourist board – called Welcome to Yorkshire. The latter body succeeded the Yorkshire Tourist Board and was to be funded by Yorkshire Forward as part of a new regionwide tourism support structure, comprising Welcome to Yorkshire and six local area tourism partnerships, one of which was Visit York (see Figure 6.1).

CTO Status, Finances, Structure and Operations

Visit York is, as an independent public–private partnership, registered as a company limited by guarantee. As shown in Table 6.4, for the 2008/2009 year the company had an income and expenditure of just over €1.7 million. Public authority grants from Welcome to Yorkshire and York City Council formed 39% of income, with the remainder derived from pri-vate sector income streams (37%) and TIC trading profits (24%). Operating budgets totalled €463,000, and the ratio of overhead to operating was €1.0–€0.37.

The governance of Visit York comprises a 14-strong Board of Directors (see Figure 6.2). The directors meet six times a year, and all are non-executives, save for the company's Chief Executive (currently Mrs Gillian Cruddas). The Visit York Board is headed by the company Chairman (currently Mr John Yeomans) who is paid an annual salary of €11,500 for the equivalent of working one day a week on company matters. All board appointments

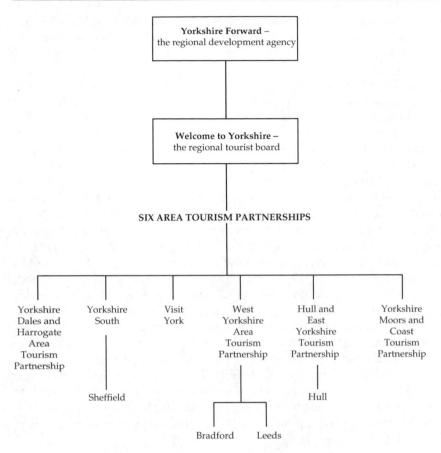

Figure 6.1 Organisation of tourism in Yorkshire

other than that of the Chairman and Chief Executive are unpaid. By profession, Mr Yeomans is a solicitor, and his former 'main job' was as a Senior Partner in a York-based firm of solicitors. He is also chairman of both the York Professional Initiative and of the official inward investment agency for the York subregion. Mrs Cruddas is a tourism marketing professional; she joined the York Visitor and Conference Bureau in 1995 and prior to this was the head of the Conference Hull tourist organisation. As Figure 6.2 indicates, York City Council nominates three directors to serve on the Visit York Board; each is a councillor representing one of the three main political parties who make up York City Council. Six other directorships draw from the ranks of the visitor attractions and hotels and catering sectors (refer to Figure 6.2) and the three that remain tap the talents and energies of a consultant, an academic and an ethnic food business support organisation. It is noteworthy that neither is the regional development agency nor the

Table 6.4 Visit York: Income and expenditure for the 2008/2009 financial year

	(€)	(€)
Income		
Public authority grants		
Local authority grant (York City Council)		351,000
Regional development agency grant (Welcome to Yorkshire)		312,000
Public authority grants subtotal	(663,000)	
Earned income		
TIC gross profit margin		419,000
Publications – income from advertising		209,000
Membership fees (York Partners)		266,000
Commissions from short break and conference bookings		114,000
York Pass gross profit margin		52,000
Earned income subtotal	(1,060,000)	
Total income		1,723,000
Expenditure		
Overhead		
Labour		901,000
Rent		117,000
Stationery, telephone and postage		72,000
IT		34,000
Other overheads		124,000
Overhead subtotal	(1,248,000)	
Operating		
Leisure tourism marketing campaigns		173,000
Business tourism marketing campaigns		54,000
Product development and research		97,000
Media relations		108,000
Business development		31,000
Operating subtotal	(463,000)	
Total expenditure		1,711,000

Source: Visit York (2010)

Directors

John Yeomans	Chairman
Gillian Cruddas	Chief Executive, Visit York
Janet Barnes	York Museums Trust
Philip Benham	North Yorkshire Moors Railway
Peter Brown	Fairfax House (co-opted and representing Civic Trust)
Cllr Sonja Crisp (Lib. Dem.)	City of York Council
Cllr Ian Gillies (Con.)	City of York Council
Michael Hjort	Meltons Restaurant
Cllr Christopher Hogg (Lib. Dem.)	City of York Council
David Martin	Consultant
Jonathan Meehan	Park Inn York
Stephen Noblett	Ethnic Food Action Group Ltd
Keith Wood	Ascot House Hotel
Dr Steve Watson	Principal Lecturer, Faculty of Business and Communications, York St John University

Observer

Roger Ranson	Economic Development Unit – City of York Council

Figure 6.2 Governance of Visit York

regional tourist board represented on the Board, despite the development agency, through Welcome to Yorkshire, being a prime source of finance and other support. In addition to her accountability to the Board of Visit York, there is in effect a parallel reporting structure in which Visit York's Chief Executive Gillian Cruddas meets on a regular basis with the Chief Executive of Welcome Yorkshire, along with the chief executives of the five other local area partnerships depicted in Figure 6.1.

The role of the Board is to determine company strategy, monitor progress and performance in the delivery and implementation of that strategy, and to ensure the company trades legally and solvently. Since the formation of the new Visit York company in April 2008, the Board (and its Chairman in particular) has developed a formal vision for tourism in the city, as well as a strategic plan for Visit York as a company covering the 2009–2012 period. Six targets are set for the York tourism sector, including 5% year-on growth in the value of tourism and securing a minimum of €57 million of investment in new tourism projects. Numbered amongst the eight targets established for Visit York are to build up company reserves and public sector financial support; to increase returns on investment from Visit York's marketing and public relations activities; to secure a 33% expansion of turnover at the company's TIC; and to grow the commercial membership from 600 to 1000.

The full-time, professional executive of Visit York comprises a team of 39 marketing and visitor servicing staff organised into five functional departments corresponding to marketing; public relations; business engagement; product development and external relations; and visitor servicing (see Figure 6.3). Regular monthly meetings of the Senior Management Team take place – comprising the departmental heads and the Chief Executive.

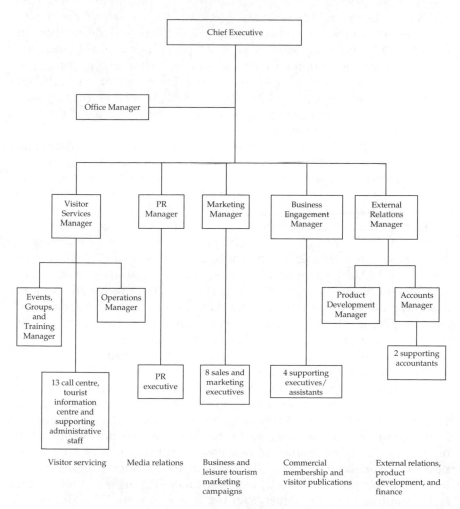

Figure 6.3 Operating structure of Visit York

Individual departments work to budgets and to financial and operational targets which are set annually (see below). Corporate progress against budget and targets is monitored at the meetings of the Senior Management Team. The principal two operational activities are marketing and visitor servicing.

The *Marketing Department* of Visit York mounts proactive leisure and conference marketing campaigns. For 2009 there were three leisure marketing campaigns: 'Shop and the city' executed throughout the year and targeting overnight stay visitors; 'I love York' undertaken over the summer months and aiming to attract day excursionists from North West England; and 'See you in York' focused on family-based short breaks, offering 'three nights for the price of two' deals, and addressing the London/South East and Midlands regions. Operating budgets are relatively small, and across the three campaigns mentioned above just €65,000 was made available in the 2009/2010 financial year to support promotions, direct mailings, e-blasts, search engine optimisation and social media marketing activities. Each campaign is evaluated by measuring the value of the resultant bookings handled directly by Visit York, as well as by KPIs covering web metrics, database growth and public relations value as estimated by reference to advertising equivalence.

The conference marketing carried out by the Visit York Marketing Department uses a conference guide, familiarisation trips, an annual 'destination showcase' event and trade and consumer exhibitions to generate 'leads' which in turn trigger sales calls and direct mailings. National association and corporate market segments are targeted, and the value of bookings placed by the company's venue finding service is monitored on a monthly basis. For the 2009/2010 financial year, this amounted to €551,000, yielding commission income to the company of €51,000. Further income of €12,000 was earned from delegate registration fees. Other activities for which the Marketing Department is responsible are the York Pass city card, enabling visitors purchasing the card to obtain discounted entry to visitor attractions, and the marketing of the company's www.visityork.org web site. For 2009, 14,000 card sales were registered, and there were 90,000 unique visitors per month to the web site.

The *Visitor Services Department* (see Figure 6.3) comprises a TIC and a linked call centre operation. Physically, the information centre is adjacent to the call centre, enabling the two services to be provided separately and therefore more effectively. At the same time, because all the 16 staff of the Department (five of whom are part time) are able to perform both information and call centre duties, a cross-over of staff is facilitated. This helps peaks and troughs in demand to be accommodated more easily, as well as increasing job satisfaction and fostering unity of purpose amongst the staff. Headline operating statistics for the 2009 year were 237,000 personal callers at the TIC, and 46,000 enquiries handled by the call centre, including

8112 individual accommodation bookings and 97 group ones. A KPI for the call centre is the percentage of telephone enquiries answered; for 2009, 97% was achieved against a target of 95%. Gross profit margin on tourist information sales for the 2008/2009 year was €419,000 (Table 6.4). The Visitor Services Department works to an annual visitor services plan. The move of both the information centre and the call centre to new and better-located premises in the spring of 2010 is expected to increase annual TIC 'footfall' by approximately 40%. Cutting-edge audio visual and other technology is being employed, and these new premises will also incorporate the offices of VisitYork at first-floor level. The capital cost of the new development is estimated at €1.1 million.

Supporting the above-mentioned marketing and visitor servicing activities are three departments: business engagement, communications and external relations and product development. At the heart of Visit York's *Business Engagement Department* (see Figure 6.3) lies the company's commercial membership scheme, called York Partners. At the time of writing, the scheme had 620 members, with accommodation providers (43%) as the largest single grouping; the remainder comprised retail (13%), restaurants and cafes (12%), visitor attractions (9%), entertainment and leisure (6%), agents (4%), transport (3%) and corporate (10%). For the 2008/2009 financial year, the membership fees paid by York Partners grossed €266,000 (see Table 6.4). According to Visit York's Business Engagement Manager, most of York's leading tourism businesses are in membership and less than 5% leave the scheme in any one year. Considerable effort is put into recruiting new members and – even more importantly – into retaining existing ones. To that end, member networking events are organised on a more or less monthly basis. The expectation underpinning membership is commercial, 'bottom' line benefit; as the Visit York's Business Engagement Manager puts it: 'Everybody is in it (viz. the membership scheme) because they want customers.'

The 620 members are featured prominently on the Visit York website, and in visitor publications, marketing campaigns and public relations activities, and from this exposure flows customers and business in the form of bookings and referrals.

The Business Engagement Department is also responsible for the production and distribution of Visit York's annual publications portfolio. Commercial members pay for advertising space in the guides which enables Visit York to raise an income line on each publication, and in so doing the company grossed €209,000 for 2008/2009 (see Table 6.4). The current portfolio comprises an A4 *York Visitor Guide* (200,000 print run) and a *York Mini Guide* (1 million print run), as well as a Christmas guide, wedding directory, conference brochure and group travel manual.

Communications activities at Visit York are spearheaded by a small, two strong *Public Relations Department* working to an annual media relations plan. The twin objectives of the plan are to generate (1) positive media coverage for York as a tourism destination, especially for short breaks and (2) a corporate profile in respect of the company's role and achievements. The work programme is labour intensive, supported by a modest annual budget of €108,000; some of this expended on a clippings service to systematically monitor media coverage, but the lion's share is used to finance press and PR activity related to the marketing campaigns and projects described above. 'Key messages' which Visit York put across under (1) seek to counter perceptions that York is 'provincial' and 'stuck in the past'; currently these cluster around the themes that to visit York is to be 'entertained', 'challenged' and 'enriched'. In respect of (2), the 'key messages' are that Visit York is a leading-edge, innovative CTO; that it is responsive to the views and needs of residents as well as visitors; and that the industry it champions is making a major contribution to the local economy. The press and PR activities undertaken by the Department centre on the following:

- Organising upwards of 100 hosted press trips a year, approximately half of which are sourced proactively: in addition, group visits of travel writers and media respondents are organised such as, for example, the British Guild of Travel Writers (BGTW) as discussed below.
- 'Feeding' journalists and other media with a regular diet of news releases distributed through the company's media database, including a quarterly *York Update* and two bimonthly issues featuring new projects/products and the city's event calendar, respectively.
- Acting as a 'one-stop shop' for media enquiries in which information, illustrations, images and other materials (e.g. destination DVD) are requested and supplied.
- Providing press and PR support to the business and leisure tourism campaigns undertaken by Visit York's Marketing Department. Here the objective is to gain coverage for the campaigns in relevant national and regional media, including 'reader's offers'.

The above activities are target driven, and performance is measured by reference to the advertising equivalence of the media coverage garnered: for 2009, this amounted to some €4.6 million.

An example of Visit York's media relations activity is the relationship it has cultivated with the influential BGTW, culminating in the hosting in York of the Guild's 2009 annual general meeting. The Public Relations Department organised a post-annual general meeting familiarisation trip for BGTW delegates attending the meeting which in due course resulted in 44 separate media items (see Table 6.5). Discounting the 11 web articles, the advertising equivalence from the remaining 33 pieces had an estimated advertising equivalence of €157,000. This represented a 2.4 rate of return on the €66,000 it cost to stage the familiarisation trip.

Table 6.5 Media coverage attributable to hosting in York the 2009 Annual General Meeting of the British Guild of Travel Writers

Type of publication	Number of published items	Example
International	3	*Sydney Morning Herald*
National newspaper	1	*Daily Express*
National consumer magazine	3	*BBC Good Food Magazine*
Regional/local newspaper	13	*Sunday Times*
Web articles	11	www.traveleditor.com
Travel publications	1	*Rough Guide to Yorkshire*
Corporate	10	BBC Radio York
Other	2	Globetrotter
Total	44	

Source: Visit York (2010)

The work of the *Product Development and External Relations Department* is fundamentally about addressing the quality of the visitor experience. This involves close collaboration with a range of stakeholders (especially York City Council) in order to encourage and grow investment across the public realm, events and festivals, the evening economy, arts, culture and heritage. Visit York seeks to respond professionally and comprehensively to strategies and to specific planning and investment issues. Examples of activities undertaken include support to events and festivals – both in marketing and event management senses – and to proposals for new hotel and attractions investments.

Conclusions

In 2007, ECM and a leading UK newspaper (the *Telegraph*) awarded York the accolades of *European Tourism City of the Year* and *Favourite UK City*, respectively. Eighty years earlier, this would have come as no surprise to Britain's foremost travel writer of the interwar period, H.V. Morton. In his classic guide referred to at the beginning of this chapter, he put the city's image and reputation on an elevated plane:

> York, Rome and London.... Those are, I think, the three most powerful place names in Europe! They ring with authority. There is rock-like assurance and reliability in the sound of them which is woefully lacking in such names as Paris, Berlin, or Brussels. (Morton, 1939: 208)

Clearly, York is not a mega-city; it is neither a capital such as Rome or Berlin, nor is it a politico-administrative hub like Brussels or an economic powerhouse comparable to, say, Milan or Frankfurt. On the other hand, its heritage and history are special, to which the praises heaped on it by Morton, the Telegraph and ECM bear witness.

Reflecting the above, it is the author's view that York's tourism is at something of a crossroads: will the city's leaders seek to build upon the city's special heritage and history and the tourist growth it has achieved since the middle of the last century so as to become a truly premier league European tourist destination, or will it, broadly speaking, be content to remain where it is now and the 'provincial' and 'turned into a heritage site' descriptors referred to at the beginning of this chapter? There is no easy or definitive answer to this question, just some pointers as set out below.

Visitor surveys conducted annually in York indicate high-satisfaction, reflecting not only the peerless and enduring appeal of what we referred to at the beginning of this chapter as York's mediaeval core, but also to supporting superstructure and infrastructure which have been introduced over the past 40 or so years: the outstanding Jorvik and National Railway Museum visitor attractions; a year round event calendar; successful pedestrianisation and park-and-ride schemes; latterly a much enhanced retail and nightlife offer; and since 1995 an increasingly proactive and purposeful CTO. The report of the Future York Group published in 2007 refers to the need fully to capitalise on York's strong reputation and to systematically exploit its potential as a tourism destination. It tasks Visit York with delivering 'transformational enhancements to York's visitor attractions; improvements to accommodation and hospitality provision within the city, in order to attract higher added value in the tourism sector'. The Group also pinpoints the need for 'place shaping' so as to imbue in the visitor a stronger sense of York as a distinctive and legible urban environment, urging York City Council to 'give priority to improving the public realm across the historic city, including paving, lighting, signage and public spaces. A higher quality of interpretation is necessary if visitors are to experience the full quality and range of the heritage offer'.

The fundamental improvements recommended by the Future York Group are being taken forward by the City Council in collaboration with the regional development agency and the York Economic Development Partnership Board. It goes without saying that realisation of the 'transformational' and 'place shaping' changes referred to above will depend upon ever more effective partnership working. In this respect, First Stop York and its successor Visit York give grounds for a measure of optimism and confidence. York City Council no longer has a vacillating and hesitant attitude towards an industry that is now an economic mainstay, and there are other key institutions and individuals outside of the municipality with whom Visit York can collaborate in increasingly productive partnerships – the ecclesiastical authorities, the members of the York Hospitality Association, York Archaeological Trust, English Heritage, the York Museums Trust, the regional development agency, the regional tourist board and – last but not least – the tourism traders and the business community generally. The concept should be that of a first choice European tourism destination achieved by enhanced partnership working across these various institutions on behalf of 'York PLC'.

In this respect, an integrative factor which is currently lacking (and which might arguably contribute powerfully to success) would be the introduction of an impactful city branding exercise, in the manner of the 'I Amsterdam' role model highlighted in Chapter 8. York has a strong image and its heritage is a distinctive competitive advantage domestically and internationally, providing a credible basis on which to develop a 'created' brand platform. In turn, this platform could act as a rallying point and as a mechanism with which to secure more effective and coordinated marketing and 'place shaping', not only within the tourism sector, but across tourism, inward investment, education, business and community. To this end, York City Council has recently appointed a design agency, Blue Sail, to help it formulate an appropriate approach and brand platform.

Whatever the future holds for York tourism, what is no longer in dispute is that it is now central to the economy, society and environment of the city; a position and importance mirrored in the openings in 2010 of Visit York's cutting-edge TIC and the city's first five star hotel – the hotel symbolically located on the site of the former Great North Eastern railway headquarters. In contrast to the railway and confectionary industries on which the city once depended for its prosperity, York's tourism is potentially there for the duration, provided that two criteria are met. First, the transformational enhancements and 'place shaping' improvements recommended by the Future York Group must be vigorously implemented, presenting the local authority and its partners with a considerable set of financial, planning and operational challenges. Second, sustainable approaches to tourism marketing and development must continue to be adopted in order to safeguard the quality of the local environment and the legitimate interests of the host community.

Part 3
City Branding

Chapter 7

The Problematic Nature of City Branding

Introduction

In this chapter we consider the topical yet much misunderstood and often controversial activity area of city branding. In many instances, what we have classified as a CMA is afforded this accountability; where it is not, it will usually work in partnership with the agency responsible for implementing the branding programme. Latterly (and especially in the Netherlands as we shall see in Chapter 8), a new breed of CMO - the city branding agency (CBA) – has emerged specifically for the purpose of advancing the city brand. This chapter begins with some context setting observations on branding products and cities. It emphasises inherent limitations and constraints, before providing an explanatory framework within which the reader will be able to understand city branding. This framework conceptualises city branding by reference to its increasingly sophisticated *structure* and to a five-stage implementation *process*. This chapter then examines how the impact of city branding can be measured, and how impact can in practice be maximised. This chapter concludes by setting out why in the author's view it is necessary to prioritise and progress this important yet problematic activity area.

On Branding Products and Cities

A city brand is a construct; a structure which is researched and designed, debated and deliberated upon, and then consciously put in place. It is not synonymous with the image, identity or reputation of a city, though people (including many practitioners, commentators and academics) frequently define it as such (see Anholt, 2007). On the contrary, a brand seeks to challenge and change 'received' image, identity and reputation. While image/identity/reputation is a sociocultural construct, branding is a business discipline. Viewed in this way, branding in its recognisably modern form dates back to the late 19th century, when it was introduced by businesses in order to advertise the products and services of an increasingly industrialised and mechanised world. For instance, in the United States, Proctor and Gamble advertised Ivory Soap in the 1890s with an 'It floats' slogan, while in the United Kingdom, Tate and Lyle did likewise for its syrup, utilising a lion logo and a distinctive green, yellow and gold pack-aging which is still in use today. In the 20th century, as Olins (2008) and others have pointed out, branding as a business discipline moved centre stage; evolving from an essentially discrete and self-contained advertising exercise into a mainstream corporate management tool and ethos. As such, branding has arguably become the central organising principle of contem-porary business organisation. Brands such as Apple, Orange, BMW, RBS, Vueling, Waitrose, M&S, Costa and Shell shape the products, environ-ments and communicative processes of these companies, as well as the manner in which they treat and otherwise relate to their employees and external stakeholders.

While the principles and practices underpinning the branding of prod-ucts are transferrable to the branding of cities, it remains the case that the process of branding cities poses a far greater set of challenges and impon-derables than it does for products such as soap, syrup, financial services and the 'ultimate driving machine'. The origins of city branding are difficult to date precisely, but logo- and slogan-led initiatives began sporadically to surface in America during the second half of the 20th century. The best known of these and one which has proved enduringly successful is *I Love New York*. Launched in 1977, it was designed by Milton Glaser working for the advertising agency Well, Rich and Green. The agency had agreed to provide a logo and a slogan on a *pro bono* basis for the State of New York to help it project a positive image of the city region. The authorities there were seeking to combat the economic and financial uncertainties then prevailing, as well as the city's reputation for urban disorder and uncleanliness. Elsewhere in America, destination branding initiatives were introduced by city convention bureaux as, for instance, with Las Vegas and *What happens here stays here*.

Pioneering European initiatives dating back to the 1980s were the *Glasgow's miles better* and *Amsterdam has it* campaigns referred to in Chapters 3 and 8, respectively. Despite their popularity, these and other municipally inspired logo- and slogan-led marketing campaigns were by contemporary standards unsophisticated, and exaggerated claims have been made on their behalves. In the early years of the 21st century, however, an altogether more powerful and ambitious concept of city branding emerged in which five key markets or audiences were to be addressed – the residents and businesses of a city, potential students and inward investors, and prospective tourists. In its new and revamped form, the city brand is frequently likened to an 'umbrella'. As such, it communicates a generic and favourable set of messages about the city, under which the 'sectoral' and targeted marketing activities of a wide range of local organisations can 'take shelter' and draw benefit – notably the 'sectoral 'marketing of the local authorities, the universities, businesses, inward investment and tourist agencies and transport authorities. Through the mechanisms of alignment and sub-branding (discussed below), 'sectoral' marketing activities can be made to reflect and reinforce the city brand.

The first example of the new breed of umbrella city brand was introduced in Birmingham (2003), followed in 2004 by Amsterdam, Glasgow and Hamburg. How the *Hamburg brand* promoted by the CBA – Hamburg Marketing – provides a platform on which to orchestrate the 'sectoral' marketing activities of the local public and private sectors is shown in Figure 7.1. The principal organisations involved consist of no less than 17 local authorities, as well as the Hamburg Chamber of Commerce, and seven public–private companies responsible for marketing selected aspects of the city's advantages and infrastructure, notably tourism, the airport, the seaport, business development, inward investment and the HafenCity urban regeneration project. Of these seven companies, some have elected to become fully fledged sub-brands of the city brand, for example, the tourist board (Hamburg Tourism) and the inward investment agency (HWF – the Hamburg Business Development Corporation). The remainder retain their own separate corporate identities, notably the Hamburg Congress and Conference Centre, the Hamburg Airport and the HafenCity development project referred to in Figure 7.1, but they nonetheless lend their support to the city brand by carrying the logo and utilising other brand materials – a practise referred to as alignment. In all of this, the crucial point to understand about the city branding activities of the CBA is that they support and supplement, but do not replace the 'sectoral' and usually highly targeted marketing activities undertaken by these other agencies.

Suffice to say that the new style of 'umbrella' brand, occupying its pivotal, orchestrating position, holds out great promise and potential. According to one protagonist, if you brand a city as successfully as BMW brand its cars, then 'the results can be far more comprehensive and economically significant and socially important than for virtually any other branding exercise' (Whitfield, 2005). Despite the topicality and alleged prowess of city branding, however, it remains the case that only a minority of cities are actively branding themselves through the conscious development and implementation of a city brand. Indeed, during the first decade of the 21st century, only 20 major initiatives are discernible across the length and breadth of Europe (see Table 7.1). Consciously engineered 'umbrella' city brands as we have discussed above therefore turn out to be the exception rather than the rule. The reasons for this merit further discussion.

Many cities with strong images/reputations/identities do not have a formal city branding platform on which they promote themselves as tourism destinations and otherwise as attractive places in which to work, study and live. This is true, for instance, of London, Paris, Rome, Florence and Venice. Paris has an image, identity and reputation suggesting

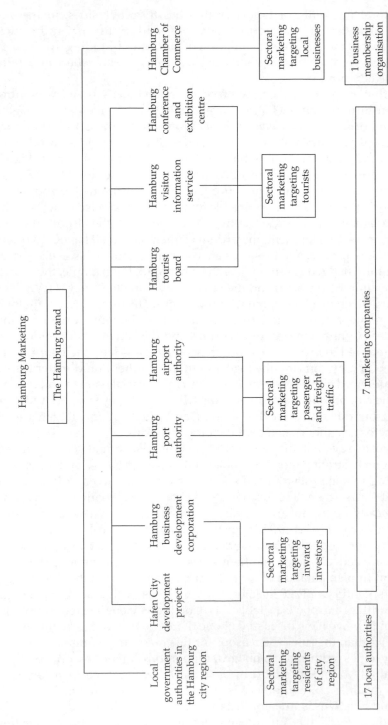

Figure 7.1 City marketing and city branding in Hamburg

Table 7.1 Brand campaigns in 20 European cities

City	Brand title	Launch	Brand authority
Amsterdam	I Amsterdam	2004	Amsterdam Partners
Birmingham	Birmingham b	2003	Marketing Birmingham
Berlin	be Berlin	2008	Berlin Partner
Belfast	Belfast B	2008	Belfast City Council
Cardiff	The Cardiff brand	2008	Cardiff & Co
Copenhagen	cOPENhagen open for you	2009	Copenhagen Brand Secretariat
Edinburgh	Edinburgh inspiring capital	2005	Destination Edinburgh Marketing Alliance
Glasgow	Glasgow: Scotland with style	2004	Glasgow City Marketing Bureau
Gothenburg	The Gothenburg brand	2009	Gothenburg & Co
Hamburg	The Hamburg brand	2004	Hamburg Marketing
Leeds	Leeds. Live it. Love it.	2005	Marketing Leeds
Liverpool	The Liverpool brand	2009	Liverpool Vision
Lyon	Only Lyon	2007	Lyon Area Development Agency
Maastricht	Everything points to the Maastricht region – to work, to live and to love	2008	Maastricht Region Branding Foundation
Madrid	The Madrid brand	2005	City of Madrid
Nottingham	Nottingham N	2005	Experience Nottinghamshire
Riga	Live Riga	2009	Riga Tourism Development Bureau
Rotterdam	Rotterdam: world port, world city	2008	Rotterdam Chief Marketing Office
Stockholm	Stockholm – the capital of Scandinavia	2008	Stockholm Visitors Board and Stockholm Business Region Development
The Hague	The Hague: international city of peace and justice	2006	The Hague City Marketing Office

romance, fine wine and cuisine and culture. In such a case, it could be argued that there is little or no need to introduce an engineered 'umbrella' city brand. What is intuitively surprising, however, is the absence of such brands in cities possessing weak or negative images. It is worth pointing out here that some cities choose an alternative approach to branding themselves. The classic ones to date have centred upon profiling a city on the back of major events and/or of iconic mega attractions. The event-led strategies of Gothenburg and Barcelona considered in Chapter 3 are examples of cities which have sought to reposition themselves in the former manner (though latterly Gothenburg has introduced a city brand). The celebrated instance of the latter is the so-called 'Guggenheim effect', whereby the Frank Gehry designed museum of contemporary art and design in Bilbao has been credited with the city's economic revival following the collapse of its iron and steel industries at the end of the 20th century. Opening in 1997, the Guggenheim Museum's striking exterior stimulated an upsurge in tourism to the Basque city and helped soften its former reputation for pollution and political violence. Other cities have sought a similar transformation of their tourism and image by creating what they hope will become an iconic mega attraction, though such an approach is high risk and courts controversy.

It is my view that the fundamental reason why engineered city brands are currently restricted to a handful of European cities is less a question of will and resourcing, and more one of the sheer difficulties of implementing them effectively – so that cities choose either to remain 'brandless' or follow the iconic statement and/or major events approaches mentioned above. In practice, there are five sets of constraints which lie at the back of this difficulty, and we consider them in the next section. Suffice to say for the moment that their combined effect is both to dissuade cities from actually going down the route of city branding, and to produce a high failure rate amongst those that do. Few city brands pass the longevity test; who, for instance, now even remembers the *Sheffield shines, Edinburgh count me in*, and *Manchester's alive* city brands introduced towards the end of the last century? These campaigns came and went with nothing much in the middle to remember them by! Indeed, as we saw in Chapter 5, the author himself has led on the introduction of no less than three city branding projects, all of which have eventually petered out in the face of these constraints, namely *Coventry inspires* (launched 1999), the *Birmingham b* (2003) and the *Nottingham N* (2005). My own experience leads me inescapably to the view that the starting point for the proper understanding and sound application of city branding is to be aware of its inherent limitations.

City Branding: The Five Constraints

The first constraint is lack of influence and control over the socio-cultural forces which ultimately shape that which city branding is ultimately seeking to transform, namely the image, reputation and identity of a city. Glasgow, for instance, has steadfastly tried to shake off its reputation for violence and murder for the best part of a century, but (as we shall see only too clearly later on in this chapter) such perceptions obdurately persist, despite city branding initiatives which advance countervailing values and images. For a CMA/CBA, there can be a profound sense of impotence when it is confronted by the random, almost anarchic mix of sociocultural factors (heavily conditioned by history and by media in the broadest sense of the word) which shape the attitudes and beliefs people have about a city. Constraint number two is the often weak relationship of city branding to other aspects of urban marketing and the city economy and its governance generally. A city brand tends to exist in a silo. It may attempt to be an 'umbrella', but in practice local organisations – marketing agencies, municipal authorities, business community and local residents – resist 'taking shelter' underneath it. Extensive adoption of the brand through sub-branding and alignment is rarely achieved. For instance, the Madrid city brand launched in 2005 has been adopted as a sub-brand by the City Council and its Madrid City Marketing Company, but there is little evidence of other sub-branding or alignment. Indeed, the Madrid Tourist Board retains its own distinctive '*Madrid about you*' corporate and destination brand.

Thirdly, there is great confusion about city branding amongst politicians, stakeholders, residents and businesses and media. To arrive at a situation in which these interests understand a city brand – let alone support it – requires powers of advocacy and persuasion which are often beyond the capacity of the CMA/CBA. The fourth constraint is funding. City branding does not pay for itself. It involves significant origination and implementation costs which the local public and private sectors are generally reluctant to fund: the former because city branding is seen as potentially courting controversy and as something which wastes public monies and lacks substance, and the latter because it is simply not their core business and does not deliver a 'bottom line' return. The fifth and final constraint is that city branding projects are difficult to evaluate. What do they really deliver at the end of the day? We pick up on this point later on in this chapter.

Armed with an awareness of these constraints, it is instructive to consider how the 20 city branding projects summarised in Table 7.1 have attempted to effect a step change improvement in how their respective cities are perceived – brands with intriguing titles such as 'I Amsterdam', 'be Berlin', 'cOPENhagen open for you', 'Leeds. Live it. Love it', 'Only Lyon', 'Belfast B', 'Rotterdam: world port, world city' and 'Stockholm – the capital of Scandinavia'.

City Brand as Structure and Process

Each of the 20 city brands summarised in Table 7.1 has a more or less similar structure made up of seven components. First, there are the *core values* underpinning the city brand – 'brand essence' as this is sometimes referred to. Nearly always with city brands, such values are deemed to be rooted in the people of the place, past and present. For instance, for the Madrid city brand developed for the Spanish capital by the international branding agency Landor, the underpinning core values arrived at were 'focused passion'. With 'I Amsterdam', the starting point once again was the people – the Amsterdammers. Three core values were identified – 'creativity', 'innovation' and 'spirit of commerce' – as we see in Chapter 8. For the 'Nottingham N', the core values were 'genuine', 'independent' and 'ambitious'. The 'Glasgow: Scotland with style' city brand is noteworthy for homing in on a single core value, namely style (Clark, 2006). Here the prime symbol of the style core value is the Glasgow-born architect, painter and designer Charles Rennie Mackintosh (1868–1928). Arriving at this particular core value was the end product of meticulous content analysis of travel reviews of Glasgow undertaken by the CMA – the Glasgow Marketing Bureau – which indicated an emergent competitive advantage for the city which clustered around style.

Components two and three of the city brand platform – *logo and slogan* – are the highly visible parts of the city brand. The logos and accompanying slogans for the 'I Amsterdam' and 'Edinburgh inspiring capital' city brands are illustrated over the page (Figure 7.2). Copenhagen has devised a flexible 'cOPENhagen open for you' logo which allows several straplines or slogans to be employed, for example 'open for business', 'open for study' and 'open for meetings'. The Hague logo (also illustrated overleaf and discussed in Chapter 8) is remarkable for the absence of slogans.

As the visible tip of the city brand 'iceberg', logo(s) and slogan(s) are critical to its success or otherwise. If they are not well received and liked, then self-evidently local organisations will be reluctant to adopt the city brand, and its usage across applications, alignment and sub-branding will be fitful. The potential for logos and slogans to engender controversy lies in part on the mistaken, but widely held, belief that they represent the entire cost of the city branding campaign. In fact, the cost is a marginal one. It also reflects the intrinsic difficulty of collapsing a city and its people, with all its facets and achievements into one symbol and a handful of words. For these reasons, city logos and slogans at and around their launches are nearly always criticised for being costly, simplistic and bland; overcoming this and achieving visibility – in formats as diverse as aeroplane fuselages, websites, posters, lapel badges and carrier bags and across community, tourism, business, events and cityscape – represents no mean challenge.

Components four, five and six are *font*, *colours* and *language*; keeping up the 'iceberg' analogy, these three components of the city branding platform are its vast but hidden underbelly. For city brands in their modern, sophisticated guise are ultimately a way of writing, colouring and speaking via font and typeface, colour palette, and tone and content

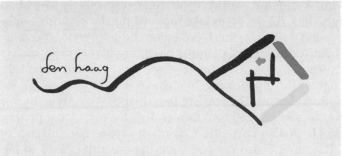

Figure 7.2 Logos for the Amsterdam, Edinburgh and The Hague city brands. (Reproduced with kind permission of Amsterdam Partners, the Destination Edinburgh Marketing Alliance, and The Hague City Marketing Office)

of voice, respectively. Last but not least – and usually the most expensive of the seven components – there are the official *city brand images* or *signature shots*. These images suffuse the marketing activities of the branding authority, and formed into a library act as a key resource to be made available to travel journalists and other media, as well as to local companies and institutions wishing to adopt the city brand. As an example, for The Hague city brand, there is an online media centre for downloading high-quality images of the city, designed to capture all its moods, emphasising the core values and messages the branding authority wishes to put across. In the 'Edinburgh inspiring capital' image library, for instance, one of the signature shots is entitled 'the Edinburgh giggle' and is presumably meant to help counteract the reputation which the Scottish capital has for being a little humourless, formal and stuffy.

All seven components of the city brand are usually brought together in *brand guidelines*; rules which set out how the brand should and should not be used, and the basis on which its usage is 'policed' by the CBA/CMA. To view an example of brand guidelines, visit www.edinburghbrand.com for the online version of the Edinburgh city brand.

So, having examined city brand as a structure, what of the process involved? There are five sequential phases. First, there is *the decision to brand* and the sometimes difficult resolution of the related issues of how it is to be funded and of who is going to be the brand authority responsible for co-ordinating the project and otherwise driving it forward. As we have mentioned already: sometimes the responsibility for the city brand will be tagged on to an existing agency, usually a CMA; increasingly, however, recourse is being made to a CBA specially created for the purposes of developing and implementing the city brand (see Table 7.1). For instance, in Holland, two CBAs – Amsterdam Partners and the Rotterdam Chief Marketing Office – are the driving forces behind the 'I Amsterdam' and 'Rotterdam: world port, world city' brands, respectively (see Chapter 8). In Edinburgh, the CBA set up to take forward the 'Edinburgh inspiring capital' city brand is called the Destination Edinburgh Marketing Alliance (DEMA). It uses this brand platform to differentiate the Scottish capital 'in an increasingly crowded marketplace by drawing on Edinburgh's key strengths and by helping to deliver a unified message …' (www. edinburghbrand.com). The work of the Alliance is overseen by a six-strong Board of Directors chaired by a former director of a global pharmaceutical company. He is also currently Chairman of the Edinburgh Convention Bureau. The other board members are the executive head of DEMA, the deputy Chief Executive of the Edinburgh Chamber of Commerce, two academics, a councillor and a solicitor. There is provision for a further five private sector appointments to the Board of Directors. Day-to-day management of the project rests with a 12-strong executive team. In contrast, the brand authority for 'Glasgow: Scotland with style' is a CMA – the Glasgow Marketing Bureau. In a small minority of cases, the branding authority is neither a CBA nor a CMA. For example, work on the Lyon city brand is discharged by a five-strong team of officers employed by the Lyon Area Development Agency.

The second phase centres upon a *brief-to-tender* for the creative development of the city brand. Preparing this can be challenging, as its scope and content may become diluted and parochial, influenced as one commentator has put it by 'the sensibilities of a multitude of stakeholders, to embrace vast compendia of previous strategic background and be informed by every imaginable study, relevant or not, conducted over the past five years' (Whitfield, 2005). Conventionally, the brief-to-tender will be issued to several design agencies and on this competitive basis a 'preferred' agency is eventually appointed. The agencies may be international, national or regional/local. For instance, the global brand designers Interbrand was appointed in June 2004 as the design agency for what became the 'Edinburgh inspiring capital' brand platform.

In the third phase, the agency commences work on *brand development*, that is, creatively assembling the seven elements of brand structure previously described, reporting throughout to whosoever is the branding authority. The development of a city brand platform requires significant resourcing, though budgets vary widely: by way of illustration, the development costs for the 'Edinburgh inspiring capital' and 'Nottingham N' city brands were €903,000 and €130,000, respectively. For the latter brand, a local design agency, Purple Circle, was appointed to advise the branding authority which in this case was the CMA, Experience Nottinghamshire. This ushered in a 16-month period of research, design and refinement. As the branding authority, the role of Experience Nottinghamshire was to manage that process, guiding and coordinating all the relevant parties and players. To this end, an Image and Branding Panel was established, drawing on communications specialists from the local authorities, universities, local media and the private sector. The Chief Executive of Nottingham City Council and the Managing Director of the local newspaper – the *Nottingham Evening Post* – were on the Panel. The Panel reviewed the various aspects of the brand platform put forward by the design agency, including the logo which turned out to be so controversial. Both the Panel and the board of directors of Experience Nottinghamshire gave wholehearted and enthusiastic sign-off to the new city brand for Nottingham early in 2005. So, when the brand was formally launched in the following month (see below) substantial support and 'buy in' had already been secured across the local public and private sectors. In particular, great care had been taken to ensure that the new brand, especially its N logo, was acceptable to both the political leadership and senior management of Nottingham City Council.

Stages one to three of the process as I have just outlined take upwards of a year and a half to complete. Stage number four – the official *launch* – is designed to get the brand off to a good start and to obtain an initial burst of favourable publicity. But securing that positive media coverage and a groundswell of community backing and acceptance is no easy rite of passage for a city brand! We shall see in Chapter 8 that the launch of 'I Amsterdam' in September 2004 at the Amsterdam Concert Hall worked reasonably well. On the other hand, the launch can sometimes backfire, as when the Glasgow Marketing Bureau unveiled its new city brand 'Glasgow: Scotland with Style' in March 2004. The launch event itself was a high profile event featuring locally born celebrities as well as media personalities. The colour palette for the new brand was dominated by black.

Problems arose next month when statistics were released showing Glasgow to be Europe's 'murder capital' as measured by per capita homicide rates. Media juxtaposed the new brand with the statistics, and came up with story after story along the lines that Glasgow's new brand was superficial and one-dimensional, and that the city's real core values were less about style and more about deprivation and murder. *The Guardian* of 11 April 2004, for example, carried a headline: 'Murder capital paints itself the wrong shade of black.' Bearing in mind the city's longstanding campaign to rid itself of its 'No mean city' image (see Chapter 3) such media report-age was little short of disastrous. Two years later, the 'Glasgow: Scotland with Style' city brand took a further blow with the publication of the book *Murder Capital* by Reg McKay – the book's front cover ironically utilising the brand colour palette!

For the launch of 'Leeds. Live it Love it' in September 2005 a champagne party was organised by Marketing Leeds, the branding authority. A high-light of this event was a film in which Leeds-born celebrities eulogised their city. The media coverage focused on the high cost of the launch event – reputedly €18,000, the alleged banality of the logo and strapline, and the embarrassing fact that Hong Kong was already using the 'Live it. Love it' slogan. Confronted by all of this, the Chief Executive of Marketing Leeds felt obliged to resign.

The launch of the *'Nottingham N'* brand early in March 2005 was an event at Newstead Abbey, the ancestral home of Lord Byron situated on the outskirts of the city, and featuring an appropriately branded hot-air balloon. Media interest was intense, and unusually for the launch of a city brand this was national and international, as well as local. Radio 5 Live conducted five separate interviews, syndicated across Radios 2, 3 and 4. Radio 4 featured the brand launch on its morning news programme 'Today', and BBC1 organised four live feeds on its UK breakfast television show. Newspapers from the Telegraph to the Sun reported on the launch. Two days later the media interest became international – from CBS Radio to the Taiwan News. The coverage – local, national and international – was uniformly critical, coalescing around the view that the former Robin Hood-based brand was to be displaced by an 'N'. Four successive features in the *Nottingham Evening Post* called for the discontinuation of the new place brand platform. As we saw in Chapter 5, the end product of this negative reportage led effectively to the cessation of the *'Nottingham N'* brand in November 2008.

After the launch, the branding authority is finally set to implement the brand. The fifth and final stage – *brand implementation* – is where the hard work really starts, and it is in this phase that many branding initiatives fail to achieve a critical mass of application and adoption. In terms of applica-tions, the branding authority (as a sub-brand of the city brand) will 'flow' the brand through all of its marketing, so that it informs its advertising, promotions, publications, web sites and merchandise/'freebies' – the t-shirts, canvas bags, lapel badges, calendars and pens. Over and above these marketing activities, the branding authority will typically seek to 'dress' the city in the logo, strapline, colours and other components of the brand, through the medium typically of banners, pennants, bus backs and sides, posters and welcome signs at transport termini. City dressing and marketing materials are used to undertake campaigns of varying degrees of intensity and sophistication, conditioned inevitably by the level of financial resource available. Following the launch of 'Glasgow: Scotland with style', for instance, the Glasgow Marketing Bureau mounted a €1.8 million campaign utilising the brand over a two-and-half-year period which included city dressing, local and national advertising, conference and short-break promotions, and press and PR activity designed to secure international media exposure.

In respect of brand adoption, the CMA/CBA or other branding authority will make it easy for travel writers and other journalists to access the signature shots via an image library, and most importantly of all will encourage local organisations to themselves become brand adopters. Occasionally it will be possible to persuade them to become sub-brands, as was the case for instance in Nottingham with Vision Nottingham (now Invest in Nottingham). The vast bulk of local organisations will, however, wish to retain their own corporate identities so the branding authority is obliged to have recourse to the much weaker form of brand adoption we have referred to as alignment. Here the brand adopting organisation will undertake to carry the logo and strapline and perhaps utilise some of the signature shots and other brand materials. In this way, the 'Nottingham N' was adopted by festivals, nightclubs, hotels, restaurants and companies such as Boots, Eversheds, Gleeds and Experian. It featured on soccer match day tickets for Nottingham Forest and Notts County; it went under ice at The National Ice Centre; and the colleges and universities used it on their websites, posters and letterheads. In Glasgow, a similar range of brand adopters were in evidence two years after the brand had been launched: the Scottish Exhibition and Conference Centre; leading city centre hotels, restaurants and department stores; the Strathclyde Partnership for Transport; and the city's educational institutions (Glasgow Marketing Bureau, 2007). For instance, the University of Strathclyde was utilising the logo and selected signature shots on its alumni publications and on prospecti.

Through applications and adoption, the branding authority seeks to give the brand visibility, all of which demands enthusiasm, creativity, perseverance and effort, and all of this comes at a considerable financial cost. In Chapter 8 we will show how successful Amsterdam Partners – the branding authority for the 'I Amsterdam' brand – has been in meeting these formidable challenges. In contrast, the failure to sustain a city brand post-launch is well exemplified by the 'Birmingham b' city brand platform.

This was launched in 2003 as a key element of a new approach to promoting the city spearheaded by the public–private partnership, Marketing Birmingham, established in the previous year (see Chapter 3). The brand platform had been produced by a local design agency, Boxer, and was premised on core values held to be reflective of the city past, present and future. Local media were equivocal about the likely impact of the 'Birmingham b', but nonetheless in the aftermath of its launch the new city brand achieved a high degree of visibility locally on posters, billboards, taxis and bannering, and a handful of agencies joined Marketing Birmingham in becoming sub-brands. However, a proactive process of adoption locally and an external marketing campaign never materialised. By 2007, Birmingham City Council's Director of Public Affairs and Communications was minded to remark that more needed to be done about the Birmingham brand. To this day the 'Birmingham b' has not been officially revised or replaced, and can best be described as being in a state of limbo. It does not feature on the municipal website nor is it used in the City Council's current 'Backing Birmingham' campaign. It survives only fitfully as the corporate brands of Marketing Birmingham, the Birmingham City Centre Partnership, the Locate in Birmingham inward investment agency and the Digital Birmingham partnership.

Having examined the process of city branding – with all its pitfalls – the next section will discuss the outcomes and impacts of city branding initiatives.

Evaluating City Branding and Maximising Its Impact

A city brand can be a powerful rallying point for local organisations to come together in order to celebrate and promote 'sense of place' from all angles and across every persuasion. In addition, there are potential economic gains to be had in providing a promotional umbrella under which the targeted sectoral marketing of other agencies is facilitated. Having said that, these economic gains are limited and difficult to quantify for the reasons specified below. Indeed, rigorous evaluation of city brands generally goes by default. It does not happen, and I am not convinced that there would be much to be gained by attempting such an evaluation. We can, of course, count the number of organisations who are sub-brands and the number of organisations who are carrying the logo and using the signature shots, but what does 'good' look like here? How many brand adopters should the brand authority seek to enlist and for how long? At Nottingham we had just over 100 one year after brand launch, but I was acutely conscious at the time both of how this had only skimmed the surface, and of how difficult it would be to secure such adoption on an ongoing basis.

Quantifying the local economic gains of a city brand when it is acting as a promotional umbrella is confronted by the methodological imponderable of how to disentangle the respective marketing influences. How do you find out how much is down to the city brand as opposed to that which is attributable to the marketing of the universities, the CTO and the inward investment agency? Branding authorities are naturally under pressure to justify brand costs by pointing to palpable economic returns, and a good example is the Glasgow Marketing Bureau (2007). The €62 million local economic benefit attributed to 'Glasgow: Scotland with style' is in effect the tourist expenditure achieved by the city over a two-year period since the brand launch in 2004. Marketing influences other than the city brand would in reality have accounted for most if not all of this growth. Brand imagery per se does not motivate tourists to visit destinations. And even if we could disentangle the respective marketing influences, would it be worth all the effort and expense? Tracking city brand awareness is problematic, too; partly for cost reasons, but also because image, reputation and identity factors get mixed up in respondents' minds with city brand influences.

In short, it is possible to demonstrate a lot of activity with a city brand, but not a precise ROI calculation. At the end of the day, a city brand is perhaps best regarded as an important 'act of faith' to which the public and private stakeholders perforce ought to be committed, and I will spell out why I think this is in fact the case at the very end of this chapter. Before that and based on the success of the 'I Amsterdam' project recounted in Chapter 8 – as well as my experience with the Coventry, Birmingham and Nottingham city brands – I summarise below how to maximise the impact of a city brand:

- First and foremost, understand city branding as a concept, structure and process; know what you are doing and try to get your stakeholders and media to understand. That is the evangelical part.
- Secondly, assemble adequate pre- and post-launch funding; at least €200,000 to develop a city brand and €300,000 per year to sustain it and give it visibility.
- Thirdly, keep the brief-to-tender simple and 'let go'; allow the design agency to be creative and resist the temptation to interfere.
- Fourthly, ensure that your stakeholders and local politicians approve of the logo and slogan(s) before the brand launch; secure maximum pre-launch 'buy in'.
- Fifthly, be prepared for the detractors; a hostile reaction to the city brand is likely from local residents, media, and the design agencies that did not win the brief-to-tender.
- Sixthly, plan for and resource the adoption process. Getting organisations to use the brand does not 'just happen'; it requires dedicated staff in post to mastermind applications and to persuade local organisations to become brand adopters.

- Seventhly, and difficult as this is, seek to embed the city brand in the business and resident community.

Suffice to say, the above-mentioned seven aspects of successful city brand management represent in total a formidable challenge!

Conclusions

Despite its topicality, we have seen that relatively few European cities have a city branding project in place, reflecting the constraints and the complexities highlighted in this chapter. While city branding is not yet a mainstream tool of urban policy, it is the case that the structure of city brands has become quite sophisticated during the past decade, and the brand authorities – be they CBAs or CMAs – have gained valuable experience in the various stages of brand implementation. As we have indicated, process and impact remain problematic. There is no tried and tested formula for successful implementation, though the 'I Amsterdam' city branding project is emerging as a role model, meriting serious study. It seems to be 'getting there' in terms both of organisational structure and operations as we shall see in Chapter 8.

Perhaps we can best sum up the future of city branding with the help of a great leader and a figure drawn from Greek mythology – Ghandi and Sisyphus. Ghandi, when asked what he thought about Western civilisation replied that he thought it would be 'rather a good idea'. Rather a good idea seems to me to be where we are with city branding today. It is work in progress to which cities on a 'needs must' basis ought to be committed, and here is where Sisyphus comes in, condemned as he was to forever push the boulder up the hill. We must keep on pushing because city branding has this great potential. First, to differentiate cities in an increasingly homogenised world. Secondly, to serve as an apolitical platform on which all the interests in a city can come together. Thirdly, to act as a promotional umbrella, providing the basis for an exemplary degree of coordinated, joined-up marketing.

Chapter 8
City Branding in the Netherlands

Introduction

Cities throughout the Netherlands are increasingly turning their attention to city branding under the guise of 'city marketing'. It can be argued that the Dutch have pioneered city branding, and there is much 'best practice' to report on in this chapter. First of all, however, we set out an overview of the peculiarly Dutch preoccupation with so-called 'city marketing'. Two city branding exercises are then considered in some detail: The Hague with its 'kite' motto and its profiling of itself as 'the international city of peace and justice'; and then Holland's capital, Amsterdam, with its leading-edge 'I Amsterdam' city brand platform. As an exemplar of best practice in city branding, 'I Amsterdam' indicates how 'city marketing is more than just a new buzzword' (Amsterdam City Council, 2004: 10).

City Marketing Dutch Style

In Holland, city marketing is a 'hot' topic: there is a heightened degree of interest in the subject, and there are countless initiatives and a growing army of academics, consultants and practitioners, reflected at a national level in the formation recently of the *Netherlands City Marketing Network*. The Network holds meetings, has introduced a city marketing awards scheme and maintains a lively level of discussion and debate utilising the business-oriented social networking site Linkedin. Indeed, Braun (2008: 29) has evidenced the first use of the term 'city marketing' in research undertaken in 1981 pertaining to the Dutch city of Apeldoorn. Dr Braun – whose doctorate appropriately enough is a study of city marketing – goes on to define it as:

> …. the coordinated use of marketing tools supported by a shared customer-oriented philosophy, for creating, communicating, delivering, and exchanging urban offerings that have value for the city's customers and the city's community at large. (Braun, 2008: 43)

As such, city marketing is a wider concept and larger undertaking than is city branding, though as Braun himself acknowledges city branding is an integral component of city marketing.

Most Dutch cities appear to have established some or other city market-ing projects, centred upon the creation and implementation of a city brand or related initiatives. Sometimes the impetus for this has come from the municipal authority and is administered directly by it – as with, for exam-ple, the *Delft City Council's Department of City Marketing*. The latter CBA was established in 2008, and comprises four local government officials who have developed a *Delft creating history* logo and strapline. Elsewhere, arms-length CMAs have been established as independent foundations. *Dordrecht Marketing*, for instance, is one such foundation, and is in the process of developing an overarching brand platform for the city region, emphasising within this platform its advantages as a tourist destination and as a place in which to live, work, visit and study. This CBA is co-located with the tourist board for the city region – WWW Zuid-Holland. Dordrecht Marketing is funded in part by the municipal authority, work-ing to an annual service-level agreement. The CBA established for the Dutch capital, Amsterdam Partners, is discussed in some detail later on in this chapter.

Reflecting the country's preoccupation with city marketing, city slo-gans and accompanying logos abound in Holland. To cite some examples, Groningen in 1990 coined the (at first mention) rather curious slogan *There is nothing beyond Groningen*; highlighting its location as the northern-most province of the Netherlands. In 1998, Almere undertook a national adver-tising campaign under the banner heading of *Everything is possible in Almere*, and a year later Eindhoven did likewise with *Ahead in technology*. Examples of other city slogans are those for Zeeland (*Feel the zeel*), Eindhoven (*Brainport Eindhoven*), Tytsjerksteradeel (*Tytsjerksteradeel really exists*), Hilversum (*Clearly visible*), Arnhem (*Made in Arnhem*), Tilburg (*Modern industrial city*) and Utrecht (*You will only find it in Utrecht*). City slogans such as these, with their supporting logos, provide a framework for marketing activities undertaken by the CBA and others. For example, Delft Marketing uses the *Delft creating history* strapline and the logo men-tioned above; here the market focus is tourists – as the CTO seeks to capi-talise on the city's heritage, as epitomised by its celebrated chinaware, the painter Johannes Vermeer and the city's links to the Dutch royal family. In contrast, the former mining town of Heerlen (population 90,000) has intro-duced a *We are Heerlen* campaign which targets local residents. On posters and banners, the residents are encouraged to speak positively about some or other aspect of local life. Promotional activities here are spearheaded by the Communications Department of Heerlen City Council within an annual budget of €50,000 specifically set aside for this purpose. The aim is to fashion 'bottom up' a new, post-industrial image for the city, with local residents acting as frontline ambassadors.

Interestingly, the Dutch new town of Zoetermeer (population 120,000) has adopted a novel approach of promoting its *Zoetermeer – leisure city* brand through user-friendly mediums attractive to young people. Part of The Hague region in the western Netherlands, Zoetermeer has abundant parkland and five leisure attractions, namely Snow World (indoor ski slope), Dutch Water Dreams (wild water rafting facility), Ayers Rock (indoor climbing), Silverdome (ice skating) and a golfing amenity – BurgGolf. In 2002, the municipal authority created a new post of *Senior Advisor City Marketing* within the Communications Department. The Senior Advisor's reporting line within the City Council is to the Director of Communications, with access to the senior councillor whose portfolio includes city marketing. The postholder works through the *Zoetermeer Promotional Foundation*; a body formed in 1994 and arms-length from the City Council. The Foundation is responsible for networking local businesses, tourism marketing and event production and marketing. One-third of the Foundation's budget comprises municipal grant, and the remainder derives from earned income streams. The 'Zoetermeer leisure city' branding initiative seeks to transform perceptions of the place: historically there had been little awareness of the city and perceptions which did exist relegated the city's role to that of a 'dormitory' suburb for The Hague. New educational and comic book materials have been produced, highlighting the city's leisure prowess and its historic centre, and these target schools and publishers. CDs enable youngsters to 'build' the city and reconstruct its ruined castle SimCity style, while 'Bob' and 'Bobette' comic characters introduce readers to the city in an informative and 'fun to read' way. Indicators of the influence of the campaign in effecting a changing image are to be found in rising levels of leisure developer interest, as well as in feedback from students and local decision makers and opinion formers.

Fully fledged city brands – as we have described them in the previous chapter – exist in the Netherlands for the city regions of The Hague, Rotterdam, Amsterdam and Maastricht. The latter project carries the strapline: *Everything points to the Maastricht region – to work, to live, and to love*. Work commenced in 2008, and is being taken forward by a CBA – the Maastricht Region Branding Foundation. A full-time managing director has been appointed to maximise adoption of the brand platform and to undertake marketing campaigns designed to create an awareness of the region as a 'single, horse-shoe shaped city with a large splendid park in the centre' (Maastricht Region Branding Foundation, 2009: 7). The Foundation itself is a noteworthy regional-level public–private collaboration, comprising no less than 20 local government authorities – 19 municipalities and the provincial authority of Limburg – and nearly 50 companies and institutions. The local authorities contribute annually to the project on the basis of a levy of €1 per resident population, while the individual donations of companies and institutions range from €5000 to over €50,000.

The Rotterdam conurbation (population 1.2 million) is Holland's second city and Europe's largest port. Its distinctive architecture, skyline and

trademark 'Swan' bridge represent a bold response to the virtual destruction of the city centre by Luftwaffe bombing in the Second World War.
Rotterdam is a cosmopolitan, modernist, 'working' city, with much of its
livelihood bound up with the reconstructed port and its ancillary industries. There is a saying in Holland: 'party in Amsterdam, live in The Hague,
and work in Rotterdam'. The desire to convey the positive attributes of
contemporary Rotterdam led the Rotterdam Development Corporation –
the estates and economic development arm of the municipal authority – to
introduce in 2004 what it was hoped would become an overarching city
brand *Rotterdam dares*. These hopes never really materialised, and in the
course of the next year the Rotterdam Economic Board (an advisory committee made up of prominent business and civic leaders) advised the City
Council to appoint a *Chief Marketing Officer* to facilitate the introduction of
a more purposeful city branding exercise. The first ever Chief Marketing
Officer, Mai Elmar, took up post in January 2006 to oversee the operation
of the City Council's *Chief Marketing Office* – the first of its kind in the
Netherlands. A logo to accompany the brand title *Rotterdam: world port,
world city* was developed by the design agency Euro RSCG Bikker at a cost
of €15,000, and the new city marketing approach was formally instituted
in September 2008. This provides for an integrative framework of messages and imagery around which the Chief Marketing Office seeks to
co-ordinate city marketing. It encourages other public and private organisations to use the brand; in particular acting as a catalyst for co-operation
across publicly funded agencies such as the Rotterdam Development
Corporation, the Port of Rotterdam Authority, Erasmus University and
the CTO, Rotterdam Marketing. Organisations as diverse as Rotterdam
Zoo, the Rotterdam Philharmonic Orchestra and the Rotterdam School of
Management are now using the logo. The activities of the Chief Marketing
Office are financed by Rotterdam City Council to the tune of €500,000 per
annum. The office is located in the Town Hall, working closely with the
City Council's Communications Department, and reports to a Supervisory
Board chaired by the Mayor of Rotterdam.

Having summarised the approach being taken in Maastricht and
Rotterdam, I will now consider in more detail the city branding projects
currently being pursued in The Hague and Amsterdam.

The Hague

The Hague conurbation (population 486,000) is currently implementing an ambitious and rather unorthodox approach to city branding. A
report in 2005 had concluded that externally the Dutch city had a weak
image and that internally there was an absence of civic pride and of style
and elegance. The report paved the way for a city marketing initiative
designed to profile The Hague around its reputation as an international

city of peace and justice. The option to establish a public–private sector partnership was discounted due to the preponderance of public sector organisations in the city – 51% of all employment in The Hague is public sector, compared with 33%, 35% and 37% for Amsterdam, Rotterdam and Utrecht, respectively. Instead, a project manager was appointed within The Hague City Council, superseded from the beginning of 2009 by the city marketing office referred to below. The fact that city marketing and the associated branding activity has been driven forward by the municipal authority has lessened the prospects for participation and financial commitment on the part of local companies and other institutions. Reflecting this, the budget set aside by The Hague City Council for city marketing purposes has been considerable (see below).

While the branding activity seeks to capitalise on the city's *de facto* position as the judicial capital of the United Nations, with its associated institutions such as the Peace Palace and the International Criminal Court, a conscious decision was taken not to use a slogan. A logo was developed by the artist Anton Corbijn for an undisclosed sum, after a brief-to-tender circulated to five advertising agencies had produced designs which were deemed unsatisfactory. With a core value of freedom and known colloquially as 'the kite', the new 'sloganless' logo was launched in November 2006 amidst the usual debate and controversy in front of one of the city's most prominent museums (the Gemeentemuseum). The launch event cost €190,000, the funding for which was split more or less equally between The Hague City Council and private sector donations.

Over the four-year period 2007–2010, responsibility for the direction and implementation of the city brand and the associated city marketing strategy has rested with The Hague City Council (AloA Consultancy, 2009). For that four-year period, a budget of €15.1 million has been made available. Initial objectives of the campaign included the development around peace and justice themes of a 'must see' museum and an iconic architectural statement, but both of these projects have made little progress. Marketing activities informed by the logo have majored on street bannering (especially flagpoles), improved signage and an 'Attractive City Programme'. A major thrust of the latter programme has been improved coordination and marketing of existing cultural events. For example, dance activities have been brought together as 'The Hague Dancing', and the June 'The Hague Festivals' has been introduced with its 'feel free to celebrate' slogan, combining classical, pop and sculpture festivals, as well as a shopping night, Dutch veteran's day and a pink Saturday event. Other activities flowing from the Attractive City Programme have been a 'be my guest' customer service initiative directed at the hospitality sector, and a variety of projects involving educational institutions. Two such projects – the creation of a 'virtual island' and another seeking to turn students into city ambassadors – have met with limited success. Press and

PR activity, on the other hand, has led to several sponsored feature articles, and there has been attendance at high-profile international events. In 2010, for instance, there will be The Hague podium at the SXSW Music and Media Conference in Austin, Texas.

In policy and budgetary terms, responsibility for The Hague's city marketing initiative resides with a Deputy Mayor – currently Alderman Frits Huffnagel – representing the *Volkspartij voor Vrijheid en Democratie* (VVD) (Peoples' Party for Freedom and Democracy). As such, he is Alderman for City Marketing, International Affairs, ICT and the City Centre. The Hague was the first city in the Netherlands to allocate at mayor level a specific responsibility for city marketing. The Hague City Council created this designation at the commencement of the new municipal administration in 2006, signalling that from now onwards city marketing would be a heavyweight, serious policy field. The Deputy Mayor's appointment in April 2006 led to the kite logo being developed, and to significant budget being earmarked for city marketing.

Day-to-day execution of the city branding project rests with a public sector CBA, a section of the City Council's Department of Urban Development called the City Marketing Office. This is headed by a city marketing manager who is assisted by three project-based positions, a management support post, and a trainee. There are two advisory groups, namely a City Marketing Process Group that links to the city government and a City Marketing Advisory Council, which is a connecting vehicle to the local business community. The former consists of senior council employees drawn from culture, international affairs, education, housing, sport, communications, urban development and the city centre. In addition, there is representation from the CTO – The Hague Marketing. As such, the Process Group is tasked with securing a coordinated interdepartmental approach across the City Council. The Advisory Council comprises 'prominent trend setters' from business, government and education sectors. It acts as a sounding board, feeding ideas and advice directly to the Deputy Mayor. Initial expectation that these sectors – through participation in the Council – would provide increasing levels of financial support has by and large not been realised. Administratively and financially, the city branding project is separate from The Hague Marketing which is responsible for promoting the city and its two seaside resorts as a tourist destination. The Hague Marketing works with the City Marketing Office, especially on events, and The Hague Marketing carries the kite logo on its website.

In conclusion, it can be seen that in The Hague city branding is now clearly positioned within the City Council. What is less evident is the sense in which the city brand has achieved a critical mass – either locally, nationally or internationally – and it is questionable whether the substantial budget deployed over the 2007–2010 period has represented value for money. Curiously, the theme of international city of peace and justice has not been utilised as a slogan, and the theme and logo fronting the campaign appear to have been developed independently of each other. Moreover, the response of local residents to the logo has been less than enthusiastic. Four years on from its inception, adoption of the city brand locally – both within and outside the City Council – appears fitful, and only recently has the www.denhaag.com web site been established to facilitate brand adoption. While the recent award by the International Festival and Events Association of a Silver Grand Pinnacle to The Hague Festivals is a high-profile expression of one successful outcome, the author's view is that an integrated and purposeful city marketing and branding initiative has still to emerge. A foundation has, however, been laid over the past four years, and as the engaging and ebullient Deputy Mayor Huffnagel is quick to point out: 'city marketing is a marathon, not a short sprint'. City marketing options for the future have been set out in a report by consultants, appropriately subtitled: 'Big talk in The Hague, or the linking element in improving The Hague's competitive position?' (AloA Consultancy, 2009: 1).

Only time will tell whether or not the investment in city branding in The Hague transcends mere 'big talk' to deliver concrete and substantial returns – for the moment the jury is out.

Amsterdam

Amsterdam (population 1.4 million) is the fifth most-visited city destination in Europe (see Chapter 2). It ranks sixth in the European Cities Monitor of Cushman and Wakefield, and fifth in the Mercer Quality of Living Index. The city is 'hip', and it oozes history, culture and tolerance; according to the *DK Eyewitness Travel Guide to Europe*, it 'is a place where beauty and serenity coexist happily with a slightly seamy side' (DK Eyewitness Travel Guides: Europe, 2006: 248). That seamy side – the city's notoriously liberal attitudes to sex and drugs – together with rising unemployment led in 1983 to the introduction of the *Amsterdam has it* slogan. This was very much the brainchild of the then Executive Mayor of the city who believed that every 'Amsterdammer has to be a seller of his town'. Twenty years later, an altogether more purposeful and sophisticated mayor-led city marketing policy was taking shape and which came to fruition as the *I Amsterdam* city brand. At its heart, there once again lay the notion of Amsterdammers providing this brand with its street-level visibility and credibility. Frits Huffnagel – who prior to occupying his current position in The Hague was the city alderman carrying the economic affairs portfolio in Amsterdam – puts it sweetly: 'I Amsterdam expresses the diversity, cohesion and individualism of all the people of Amsterdam' (Amsterdam City Council, 2004: 7).

The process of developing a new city marketing approach began in December 2002. Management consultants – Berenschot – were 'parachuted' in to undertake an assessment of Amsterdam's competitive strengths, and an audit of the way it marketed itself as a city. Their report published one year later predictably concluded that Amsterdam 'needed to intensify its city marketing efforts' (Berenschot, 2003: 2). It alluded to a plethora of organisations with a stake in city marketing, to a fragmentation of effort and funding, and to an absence of direction and effectiveness. Relationships between the city government and Amsterdam's leading companies were poor. There was a set of unrelated visions and marketing materials, and a lack of meaningful cooperation between the key players – Amsterdam Promotions, the CTO, the official cultural and sporting agencies and the marketing arms of the various transport bodies (rail, airport, canals, harbour and cruiseport). Indeed, with characteristic Dutch forthrightness, Berenschot went as far as saying that 'the city and these middle ground organisations (most existing thanks to city subsidies) regularly fall in and out with each other' (Amsterdam City Council, 2004: 29). It called on Amsterdam City Council to 'take the lead to develop one vision of the Amsterdam brand', suggesting that the Council's own 'house style might serve as the basic start position' (Amsterdam City Council, 2004: 15).

The Berenschot report laid the foundation for an ambitious and ground-breaking initiative in which a new city brand was developed alongside a novel partnership approach towards its implementation. No less than 16 strands of competitive advantage were matched against seven target audiences. After over a year of research, interviews with Amsterdammers, and deliberations between Amsterdam City Council and the various stakeholders, the year 2004 witnessed three important milestones. First, the establishment, on 4 March 2004, of an independent public–private partnership to act as the delivery mechanism for the new city brand – Amsterdam Partners. The high-powered management board of Amsterdam Partners was to be chaired by a leading representative from the private sector, Willem Stevens, the Senior Counsel serving Baker & McKenzie. The other board members were the Alderman for Economic Affairs (Frits Huffnagel), the President of the Amsterdam Chamber of Commerce, the Mayoress of Almere City Council and the Chief Financial Officer of Wolters Kluwer. The second milestone, in April 2004, was the approval given by the cabinet of Amsterdam City Council to an official policy framework for city marketing which delineated the respective roles and responsibilities of the Council, Amsterdam Partners, the various 'sectoral' city marketing agencies and the city's leading companies and institutions. This framework permitted an arrangement under which Amsterdam Partners policed, managed and otherwise directed the implementation of the brand under license from its owners – Amsterdam City Council. It also enabled Amsterdam Partners to establish agreements in which it set up cooperation arrangements with eight agencies, namely the Amsterdam Airport Area, Amsterdam Uit Bureau (the Amsterdam cultural bureau), Amsterdam

Tourism and Convention Board, Amsterdam Centre for Architecture, Topsport Amsterdam (the Amsterdam sports council), KennisKring (a knowledge and information transfer clearing house), Amports (the port authority) and Amsterdam Cruiseport. As organisations collectively exerting a huge influence on the manner in which the city is promoted, these so-called 'covenant partners' agreed to adopt and otherwise give heavyweight support to the new city brand.

The third milestone was the launch of the 'I Amsterdam' brand on 23 September 2004. The 'good and great' of the city assembled at the Amsterdam Concert Hall to take in presentations, a book and exhibition featuring specially commissioned photographs of Amsterdam, and the brand website www.iamsterdam.com. A second version of the site went live in 2008, representing a remarkable partnership achievement in that it embodied and combined the strengths of seven 'sectoral' marketing organisations:

- The Amsterdam Tourism and Convention Board (ATCB)
- The Amsterdam Uit Bureau
- Amsterdam Top City (a clearing house and facilitator of inter-agency collaboration)
- Amsterdam in Business (the city region investment board)
- The Expat Centre (the regional service bureau for expats and foreign residents)
- The Communications Department of the municipality
- Amsterdam Partners (the branding authority)

Effectively each of these organisations became a sub-brand of 'I Amsterdam', giving an impressively joined up 'look and feel' throughout their various marketing endeavours. The portal itself is nowadays receiving monthly in the region of 200,000 unique visits.

Arguably even more impressively, brand adoption soon became evident within the municipality. Amsterdam City Council systematically employed the city brand to fashion a uniform house style across 44 urban districts and 45 municipal departments – from museums to tax offices. As a result, 'I Amsterdam' is now evident on trams, vans, signage, posters, stationery, brochures, presentations and fact sheets. As the Director of Amsterdam Partners could remark:

> The Council's house style is a perfect point for the development of a city marketing style for Amsterdam. I Amsterdam now links all the Council's marketing initiatives with those of entrepreneurs in the city, and ensures the desired consistency and recognisability. (Berenschot, 2003: 17)

The reference to entrepreneurs in the city was no idle boast. As at the time of writing, the 41 members of the Supervisory Board of Amsterdam

Partners reads like a 'who's who' of Amsterdam's corporate prowess, with names such as the Schiphol Group, Wolters Kluwer (information services), ABN–AMRO (banking), Phillips Global (electronics), ING Real Estate, Nuon (energy), Heineken (brewing), the Dutch Bank, KLM, the University of Amsterdam and the soccer club Ajax – the list is almost endless.

Amsterdam Partners is officially the CBA for the Amsterdam metropolitan area. Constituted as an independent public–private foundation, its five-strong management board is currently chaired by the head of corporate affairs for the Schiphol Group. The other members are senior-level appointments drawn from Wolters Kluwer, the Amsterdam Chamber of Commerce and the city councils of Amsterdam and Almere. Reporting to the management board is a team of 12 employees who on a day-to-day basis take forward the 'I Amsterdam' city brand. For 2008, Amsterdam Partners worked to a budgeted income of €2 million, nearly all of it (96%) derived from partner contributions – one-half coming from local authority subvention and the other from 'bite-size' donations of €20,000 from no less than 45 prominent Amsterdam companies and institutions committed to promoting an enhanced image of the city region (Amsterdam Partners, 2009). The core purpose of Amsterdam Partners is 'to strengthen the Amsterdam brand in the eyes of relevant city marketing target groups' within the framework of the three competitive advantages and brand values that 'make Amsterdam stand out ... creativity, innovation and business acumen' (Amsterdam Partners, 2009: 4).

For the year 2008, Amsterdam Partners incurred a marketing expenditure on operation of €1.6 million, addressing three target audiences – international decision makers, tourists and the city region's own inhabitants. Much of the marketing activity is centred on the splendid portal web site to which previous reference has been made: www.iamsterdam.com portrays the 'I Amsterdam' look and feel, while acting as a one-stop shop for residents, investors, businesses and visitors seeking information about the city region and offering supporting transactional and reservation services. A small but significant portion of the marketing budget (4%) comprises networking expenses. This activity is coordinated by the CBA's Network Project Manager and seeks through meetings, an annual outing and other informal contacts to maximise partner commitment to the city brand. In part, this is about maintaining and expanding the local authority subvention, as well as the 'bite size' funding contributions from companies and other institutions Equally, if not more importantly, it is about strengthening relationships with the various partners so as to deliver additional 'off the balance sheet' activity in support of the 'I Amsterdam brand'. Networking encourages public and private sector partners to themselves utilise the city brand in their own media and marketing activities, becoming what we referred to in Chapter 8 as brand adopters. Brand adoption by partners takes many forms: deploying the logo and brand images on canal boats, screens at Amsterdam airport, and

JCDecaux outdoor display cases, and at high profile venues such as the Amsterdam Arena and the Ajax football ground. It leads Heineken to align its Amstel 'One Dam Good Beer' advertising campaign to the city brand. In this cooperation with Amsterdam Partners, the 'I Amsterdam' logo appeared prominently in commercials and at the New York launch of the campaign on Amsterdam Avenue. In these and many other ways, the city brand becomes ever more impactful at no or little cost to Amsterdam Partners. Effectively, adoption of the brand enables it to expand marketing activity beyond that expensed from within its own relatively modest budgets.

The brand-related marketing undertaken directly by Amsterdam Partners is creative and innovative. For instance, a recent campaign sought to exploit the annual Queen's Day holiday by inviting residents and visitors to 'party' in the city, utilising posters depicting world leaders seemingly representing Amsterdam, for example American Secretary of State Hilary Clinton sporting an orange afro wig! Promotional activity makes use of Amsterdam icons – from Rembrandt through to Ajax football club and a popular Dutch disc jockey. Guerrilla marketing has cleverly utilised striking Amsterdam-related 'It takes twenty five words to change the world' testimonies. Bannering is evident in the city, and three-dimensional 'I Amsterdam' letters are placed in high footfall locations. A range of eye-catching 'I Amsterdam' merchandising has been developed which is now turning over €500,000 per annum. There are 'meet and greet' city stewards at Central Station, and 'Iambassadors' have been recruited from the ranks of journalists and the creative industries. A sizeable chunk of Amsterdam Partner's marketing budget (32%) is devoted to giving visibility to the 'I Amsterdam' city brand at major events both in and outside of the Netherlands – festivals, congresses and sporting championships. In this respect, 40 events were linked to 'I Amsterdam' in 2008, including Amsterdam International Fashion Week and Dream Amsterdam.

Amsterdam Partners targets its international communications and marketing activities on 11 cities – New York, San Francisco, Los Angeles, Boston, Berlin, Barcelona, Bombay, Beijing, Shanghai, Guangzhou and Tokyo. The aim is to position the city region as an ideal location for companies to base their European headquarters. In a collaboration with the inward investment agency (Amsterdam in Business), a glossy 'quality of life' magazine 'Proud' is published for distribution to opinion formers and decision makers, and media campaigns are undertaken to profile Amsterdam internationally – a recent one majored on a 'good ideas grow big in Amsterdam' theme.

Conclusions

Every city in Holland seems to want to do something to manage its identity and reputation, turning to marketing and branding techniques in a quest variously to boost the resident 'feel good' and to attract tourism and other 'footloose' audiences – notably students and inward investors. The term 'city marketing' has been used in the Netherlands for quite some time now as a convenient way to categorise all of this activity, though the categorisation itself belies the complexity and the three more or less distinct marketing and communication strands which exist. First, there are initiatives to promote civic pride of the type described above taking place in Heerlen, and nearly always undertaken by the municipal authority. Secondly, we have the destination marketing undertaken on a city or city region basis by CTOs such as Rotterdam Marketing and the ATCB. Thirdly, there is city branding where an engineered vision for a place is translated into an overarching identity, providing an umbrella under which the 'sectoral' marketing of city businesses, municipalities, universities, tourist boards and others can be given focus and made more effective.

In respect of city brands, there is a clear sense in which Amsterdam is emerging as the 'leader of the pack', with 'I Amsterdam' beginning to overcome the characteristic constraints and limitations surrounding this particularly problematic form of marketing and communication activity. The web portal www.iamsterdam.com is an exemplary partnership construct, and the marketing activity carried out by Amsterdam Partners is inspired. The City Council 'I Amsterdam'-based house style is a masterstroke, and the networking of partners to provide budget and 'off the balance sheet' contributions to further boost 'I Amsterdam' marketing has no equal with which the author is familiar. Moreover, the brand values – creativity, innovation and spirit of commerce – appear to tie in with what the city and its institutions and people can actually deliver upon. Organisationally, the case of 'I Amsterdam' indicates that a city brand is only likely to succeed where a CBA is created specifically to act as custodian of that brand, winning for itself decisive and far-reaching influence. In this respect, Amsterdam Partners is exemplary as a delivery mechanism, 'walking the talk' of the stretching target it sets for itself which is simply to 'be good and tell it'.

Postscript

A curious and interesting manifestation of Dutch humour and of the impact 'I Amsterdam' is having is the existence of a counterbrand 'Ai Amsterdam', complete with its own www.ailoveamsterdam.nl. For information, 'Ai Amsterdam' is pronounced the same as 'I Amsterdam', but 'Ai' in Dutch means pain!

Part 4

Conclusions

Chapter 9
Whither City Tourism and City Tourism Organisation?

Introduction

This chapter begins by drawing together multifarious strands from those that have preceded it in the form of a résumé. It then appraises city tourism and city tourism organisation from what I believe is the watershed of 2010 where both stand at something of a turning point. Finally, the perspective shifts to the future, and to what city tourism and city tourism organisation will look like in 2020, focusing as much on what in the author's view are likely to be the continuities as the discontinuities.

Résumé

I began this book with a preface setting out six reasons for writing it. In the first chapter, I presented a typology of city tourism organisation, before examining the evolution of city tourism as both a market and as an organisational, supply-side collaboration of the local public and private sectors. We saw how a sustained and unprecedented 'boom' in city tourism took place over a 16-year period 1990–2006, with the rate of growth halted by the first signs of economic recession in 2007. Over the previous century and a half, a 'patchwork quilt' of city tourism organisation had established itself. Reflecting the fact that tourism is essentially a localised phenomenon in respect of its impact and administration, the city tourism organisation which emerged throughout Europe from the mid-19th century onwards reflected parochial needs and circumstances. Although in Eastern Europe city tourism organisation remains centred on local government, elsewhere a pervasive trend became discernible in favour of what I have called the public–partnership model. There is a natural logic to the model – financially, structurally and operationally – and even in Eastern Europe the harbingers of public–private partnership are lately emerging.

In Chapter 2, city tourism was examined as a market force so as to give the reader a flavour of its contemporary significance commercially and economically. A particular and very practical emphasis was placed on how city tourism is measured; both the volume and value of the industry and the performance of CTOs/CMAs. Four kinds of measurement parameter were identified, namely industry, community, marketing and benchmarking. In this chapter, I concluded that within city tourism organisation measurement and the associated intelligence gathering and reporting procedures have been afforded an insufficiently high priority. This is especially marked in relation to benchmarking and to the evaluation of the marketing campaigns which are central to the operational activities of CTOs and CMAs. Drucker's 'if you can't measure it, you can't manage it' maxim is pertinent here, with benchmarking and the evaluation of marketing campaigns representing 'work in progress' for the majority of CTOs and CMAs.

Chapter 3 appraised the dynamics of city tourism development, mapping out the respective roles and responsibilities of the local public and private sectors, before considering in turn five European cities who have successfully fashioned for themselves a more positive post-industrial image as well as a buoyant tourist sector. The approaches of Barcelona, Birmingham, Dublin, Glasgow and Gothenburg drew attention to two critical success factors: first, the need for a focused and autonomous public–private delivery mechanism with which to vigorously market the city; and secondly, a city government committed to supporting and resourcing the tourism and 'imaging' strategy. City government must 'be there': from the mayor or leader downwards; across planning, development, infrastructure and communications; and for the entire duration of the strategy. The formula for success in urban tourism may be summarised as arms-length marketing on a bedrock of 'full-on' commitment from the city administration. The other side of the coin is that tourism fails to realise its potential in situations where the commitment of city government is lukewarm, partial and fitful; he who dabbles, prevaricates and waivers in tourism and in the fostering of city image rarely wins out over the medium to long term.

Chapter 4 established a framework of concepts within which to understand the structure and functioning of city tourism organisation. Referring to the public–private partnership model, it distinguished the 'amateur', volunteer governance from the 'professional', remunerated executive, exemplifying by reference to the CTOs for Vienna, Oslo and Valencia. The structures sketched out in Chapter 4 are noteworthy for the sense in which the points of difference are outweighed by the commonalities; the governance and executive of the VTB is recognisable in those established for Valencia Tourism and Visit Oslo. The rest of Chapter 4 identified and commented upon the principal operational programmes and activity areas which characterise city tourism organisation, using case material drawn from the innovative and well-resourced VTB whose historical evolution we had previously traced as part of Chapter 1. As with the structures for governance and executive, the template of VTB marketing, communications and visitor servicing activities appraised in Chapter 4 is more or less

discernible in CTOs and CMAs across the length and breadth of Europe –
from Visit Reykjavik and Visit York to the Antwerp Tourism Department
and the Opatija Tourism Office. What is noteworthy about the Vienna case
is the scale, professionalism and effectiveness of the operational activities.

The focus of Chapter 5 moved from structure and functioning to 'start
up' and leadership, as it follows the author's own experience over a
19-year period (1990–2009) in the English cities of Sheffield, Coventry,
Birmingham and Nottingham. Eight 'building blocks' essential to successful 'start up', and nine 'lessons learned' in respect of leadership were highlighted. Amongst the dimensions highlighted as critical to success were
the following: the stature and abilities of the chairman and CEO and the
nature of their relationship to each other; the attitude as well as professional capabilities of staff; the provision of sound and timely management
information (easily said, but not so easily achieved); the requirement to
measure marketing effectiveness; and a CEO mindset which I characterised as 'retaining passion and losing emotion'. The framework of structural, operational, 'start up', and leadership considerations adumbrated in
Chapters 4 and 5 was then brought together and deployed in Chapter 6 in
the form of a city case study, examining one of Britain's leading heritage-
based tourism destinations, York. In this chapter, the work of the CTO –
Visit York – was examined and contextualised by reference to both
demand-side and supply-side considerations.

Chapters 7 and 8 were devoted to city branding: a little understood, but
highly topical and ultimately problematic activity area; one which is integral to city tourism while at the same time embracing wider domains,
concerns and players – notably what we referred to as CBAs. Chapter 7
presented an overview, tracing the evolution of branding principles as
these have been applied to industrial and commercial products and then
to cities, beginning with Amsterdam and Glasgow in 1983. It set out the
factors which in practice constrain the effectiveness of city branding as a
tool of urban marketing and policy and, in turn, limit its actual and practical application to a minority of European cities. Reference was then made
to the experience of 20 cities where consciously engineered brand plat-
forms had been introduced during in the first decade of the 21st century,
enabling city branding to be appraised and understood as a structure
made up of seven components and as a process comprising five distinct
phases. This chapter concluded by stressing the potential and promise of
city branding, paving the way for Chapter 8 and a case study of city branding in the Netherlands. Here, the practice of city branding was set within
the context of the current vogue for 'city marketing' which characterises
that country. In Amsterdam and The Hague, two of the country's leading
approaches were compared and contrasted, with the 'I Amsterdam' city
brand emerging as a model of 'best practice'.

Having summarised all that has gone before, in the remainder of
Chapter 9, the author will attempt to 'take stock'; first, by reference to the

'here and now' of 2010 and the watershed reached by city tourism and city tourism organisation, and secondly, by speculating as to how things will be 10 years 'down the line' in 2020.

The Watershed of 2010

It is all too tempting and sometimes too easy to conclude a book at some or other watershed, but in the cases of both city tourism and city tourism organisation, the author considers it well justified. Taking city tourism first, we discussed in Chapter 2 how the 'boom' in urban convention, events and short-break traffic started to come to a close in 2007 amidst the first signs of global economic recession. In that year, the growth in bednights recorded for Europe's leading cities was just 3%, compared with the 8% and 7% figures registered in 2005 and 2006, respectively. In 2008, the total market for European city tourism as measured by bednights showed little or no year-on growth at all, and in the first quarter of 2009, it dramatically contracted by –7% (ECM, 2009, 2010). Tentative signs of recovery are evident at the time of writing, and it is important not to overstate the magnitude of the recession-induced flattening and then contraction of the market for city tourism. However, the optimism and confidence which had been engendered by the sustained and often double-digit growth rates which had characterised the 1990–2006 years has been dented. Growth no longer assured and assumed has latterly prompted more cautionary outlooks amongst city tourism chiefs and industry leaders, and with it comes a sense of being at a watershed.

For city tourism organisation, the ending of the 'boom' years meant reporting on declining volume and turnover: a markedly different and more difficult context within which to satisfy public and private sector stakeholders anxious for the 'payback' referred to in Chapter 5. When trip, bednight, expenditure and occupancy statistics are continuously 'on the up', stakeholders are in general quiescent, and the somewhat naive assumption is made by them that somehow or other the CTO/CMA is responsible for all (or a substantial part) of the annual growth being registered. The reverse situation lends itself to doubts, and public and private sector stakeholders typically start to ask questions such as the following: with our own budgets and finances constrained by recession and the need to cut costs, do we have sufficient funds to continue with our financial support to the CTO/CMA?; is the CTO/CMA really putting 'heads in beds'?; why is this or that marketing opportunity not being capitalised on? This questioning against value for money, cost effectiveness and ROI criteria is one factor contributing to CTOs/CMAs currently standing at a watershed. Furthermore, it homes in on the 'Achilles heel' identified in Chapter 2, in that city tourism organisation has a patchy and somewhat disappointing record in terms of measuring its marketing effectiveness.

Another factor – one once again aggravated by the recent economic recession – is the financial vulnerability of city tourism organisation as highlighted in Chapter 5. Only a handful of European CTOs/CMAs are stable in the sense that they are appropriately geared, have an underpinning financial strategy and possess adequate reserves. We saw in Chapter 5 how financially exposed city tourism organisation is due to its dependence on discretionary municipal subvention, external grant regimes which come and go, and hard won and invariably fluctuating levels of trading income and private sector sponsorship, fees and other contributions. Of the minority of CTOs/CMAs who are financially stable, for example those for Vienna and Geneva, there is a firm foundation of funding support derived from tourist taxes levied on the industry. Elsewhere, both local and national governments remain opposed to the introduction of hypothecated tourist taxation, and as a consequence the greater part of city tourism organisation exists in a state of financial instability. The outcome of recession has been to worsen this instability: partly because many city government and other public sector budgets are under threat and being pruned as we emerge out of recession, but also because private and earned income streams have self-evidently been put under pressure. Financially speaking, therefore, city tourism organisation stands at a watershed.

A pertinent market-related factor requiring consideration here is social media and how it, in turn, is contributing to city tourism organisation being at a watershed. I referred in the preface to a likely paradigm within a paradigm shift in which increasing use is being made of social media as a way of reaching and communicating with key audiences. Social media hold out a prospect of being able to create new visitors as part of a 'bottom-up' interaction between the CTO/CMA and its various customers and clients, as opposed to a conventional 'top-down' communications and marketing exercise based on advertising, promotions and mailings, and backed up by supporting print and press and PR activities. There is a dichotomy opening up between 'traditional' and 'new' social media-based approaches, with the latter supplementing and even replacing the former. Professionals working in city tourism are trying to chart the correct course of action within this paradigm within a paradigm shift. Unlike the 'traditional' marketing practices, there is at present no tried and tested formula for effectively deploying social media so as to secure bookings, conversions and ROI, though the tantalising prospects of success in this field are there for all to see. Here lies a further set of uncertainties and dilemmas which represent another dimension to the watershed referred to above.

A fourth and final dimension lies in the branding exercises discussed at length in Chapters 7 and 8, and which aim to provide an 'umbrella' framework within which a city promotes awareness of its competitive advantages across tourism, inward investment, education, lifestyle and culture. Properly and effectively implemented, such branding initiatives enable a range of 'sectoral' marketing strategies (tourism included) to be better coordinated and otherwise made more effective. Experience – positive and negative – suggests the responsibility for implementing a city brand should rest with a specially constituted CBA, along the lines of Amsterdam Partners as highlighted in Chapter 8. However, Amsterdam Partners, and its 'joined up' relationships with the Amsterdam Tourism and Convention Board, other city marketing agencies, and the local authorities, is very much the exception rather than the rule. Elsewhere, the relationship of the CTO/CMA to city branding tends to be less clear and satisfactory. Where there is not a city branding project in place, then self-evidently there is no relationship whatsoever. Where a city brand is implemented by what we have referred to as a CMA, then its widespread adoption tends to be constrained because the brand is perceived as being 'tourism' and the preserve of the tourist agency – as opposed to being for the city as a whole. In those circumstances where a CBA has been established, then with the exception of Amsterdam the linkages between the city brand and the CTO appear rather tenuous and ill-defined, for example consider the case of the Rotterdam city brand and Rotterdam Marketing discussed in Chapter 8. What this all boils down to in terms of city tourism organisation being at a turning point is that (Amsterdam aside) there is a generally ambiguous and weak relationship between city branding and the destination marketing activities undertaken by city tourism organisation.

Reaching a watershed in 2010 is therefore the end product of how the global recession of 2007–2009 brought to an end a 16-year 'boom' in city tourism which, in its turn, brought into sharp relief uncertainties pertaining to four critical dimensions of city tourism organisation, namely (1) measuring its operational performance and, in particular, quantifying rate of return on marketing investment, (2) its financial instability, (3) the extent and the manner in which it ought to embrace social media as the basis of its marketing activity and (4) its generally weak and ambiguous relationship to city branding. To predict the scope and direction of movement from the watershed arrived at in 2010, it is important to set against these current uncertainties the proven and enduring strengths of city tourism and city tourism organisation, and it is to both uncertainties and strengths that I now turn in attempting to predict the shape of things to come.

Ten Years on and 2020: Continuities and Discontinuities

Crystal ball gazing is self-evidently hard to do successfully, as there is no possible way of knowing exactly what will happen in the future. Based on knowledge and experience, however, speculation about what is likely to obtain come the year 2020 nevertheless has its place, and at the same time it is an apposite note on which to end. Whether it has value, only time itself will tell.

From the demand side of the equation, city tourism came of age in the latter half of the 20th and early 21st centuries. For the city of York, for instance, we showed in Chapter 6 how a first wave of demand unfurled gently but steadily after the Second World War. Earlier in this chapter, we referred to the 1990–2006 'boom' in city tourism with its sustained and impressive year-on growth rates. To keep with the analogy, the period 1990–2006 represented the unleashing of a second much more powerful wave, transforming city tourism into the truly potent market force it nowadays represents. Notwithstanding the 2007–2009 economic recession and the associated 'dip' in city tourism volume and value, market intelligence and returns for the second half of 2009 and the first part of the 2010 year indicate recovery and a return to growth-related scenarios (ECM, 2010), albeit not at the levels experienced between 1990 and 2006. Cities have become the pre-eminent focus of urban travel, as reflected in easy accessibility, a plethora of 'attractors' generating visits in their own right, and a huge supporting infrastructure of retail, accommodation and catering. Moreover, the untapped market potential in emergent source markets such as India, Russia and China points to the demand for European city tourism recovering in the next decade to significantly surpass pre-recession levels by the year 2020.

It is the author's view that city tourism organisation will continue to be a feature of Europe's institutional landscape because there is a template of demonstrably successful activities – from press visits and travel trade familiarisation through to attracting conferences and short breaks and providing information. For these and all the other activities making up city tourism marketing, there is a more or less enduring need. Undertaking such activities in a purposeful, well-resourced, and sustained manner not only generates wealth and prosperity through tourism; it is also the single most cost-effective way of raising the profile of a city and improving its reputation and image. This has been the case since time immemorial: Richard 'Beau Nash' who was employed by the spa town of Bath during the 18th century as its 'Master of Ceremonies' is the precursor of today's CTO – Bath Tourism Plus. Over time the form and content of the marketing, communications and visitor servicing activities has undergone change, sometimes dramatically so as with that occasioned by the web and internet late on in the 20th century, but the fundamental needs being satisfied remain constant. Nash created and serviced visitors and safeguarded city reputation, just as 300 and so years later Bath Tourism Plus is doing today.

Over the next decade, I am inclined to believe that the public–private partnership model of city tourism organisation will become ever more pronounced because of its natural logic and powerful operational, organisational and financial advantages. Just as in 2003 – when this logic and these advantages persuaded the Bath and North East Somerset Council to relinquish control of tourism in order to establish Bath Tourism Plus as an independent public–private partnership – I expect throughout Europe we will witness similar administrative 'migrations'; as cities which have hitherto retained local authority administered tourism move to a public–private partnership form of organisation.

In line with this, I predict city tourism organisation in 2020 will be 'fitter', financially more stable and rationalised. Logic would dictate that the tools with which to monitor effectiveness outlined in Chapter 2 will in the course of the next decade be deployed more systematically than has hitherto been the case. Securing an appropriate and proven rate of return on marketing investment and achievement of explicit KPIs has only lately become a mainstream concern for the governances and senior management of CTOs/CMAs, as we saw in Chapters 2 and 5. Throughout the next decade, this concern will loom ever larger and spread widely, leading to 'fitter' (i.e. more responsive and cost efficient) operations.

I foresee greater financial stability obtaining within city tourism organisation because there will be proportionately less reliance on the public sector in the form of discretionary municipal subvention and external grant regimes. Budgets will come to be dominated by earned and private sector income sources, as the locus of public and private responsibility for funding city tourism organisation shifts away from the public purse. I hope in this respect to see more frequent recourse being made to hypothecated tourist taxes levied on the industry. It is fitting that the main beneficiaries of tourist spending – the accommodation providers, shops, restaurants, attractions and transport operators – should be the principal funders of city tourism organisation. Financial gearing dominated by earned and private sector monies will mean governance by the private sector and a preoccupation with ensuring appropriate rates of return on marketing investment. He who pays the piper calls the tune!

Having said that city tourism organisation will endure in 'fitter' and more stable modes, I expect in 2020 to see fewer CTOs/CMAs, with rationalisation occurring across two fronts. First, some CTOs/CMAs will have their life supports turned off when confronted by reduced financial support from the public purse; others will be closed down because they are demonstrably inefficient and failing as delivery mechanisms; and some will expire due to the fact that there is an insufficient critical mass of tourist industry support and competitive advantage in terms of the city's tourist offer. Rationalisation will be especially marked in relation to city government-based CTOs/CMAs as opposed to those which have adopted the public–private partnership form of organisation. Indeed, during the next decade I expect public sector tourism as a whole to diminish significantly at all geographical levels – national, regional and local. Tourism departments located within city administrations will become an endangered species (along with publicly funded NTOs and RTOs) precisely because their cost-effectiveness is highly questionable. A second strand of rationalisation will see CTOs amalgamated with CBAs, inward investment and business promotion agencies, offices undertaking film location and events units. Rationalisations of this kind hold out the promise of improved coordination and service delivery as well as cost-cutting economies of scale, and they are already being planned in Lulea, Uppsala, Amsterdam, London, Warsaw and Edinburgh. More will follow.

A fundamental continuity into the next decade will be the ascendancy of the web and internet as the medium within which marketing connects audiences and customers with cities. By 2020, city tourism and marketing organisations as intermediaries will in essence have become 'emediaries'; implementing 'bottom-up' web- and internet-based strategies rooted in social media. The form as opposed to the content of the destination marketing first undertaken by the author in the early 1990s will by 2020 have become more or less unrecognisable.

A penultimate conjecture is that in 2020 the culture and values underpinning city tourism organisation will be ones grounded in sustainability. To date, tourist chiefs and CTOs/CMAs have paid much 'lip service' to the pursuit of sustainable forms of marketing and development. Bath Tourism Plus, for instance, prides itself on its commitment to sustainability and its silver award under the Green Tourism Business Scheme. To be sure, there has latterly been some 'movement' in the sense of CTOs/CMAs instituting environmentally friendly office practices, encouraging industry operators to join green accreditation schemes, and themselves undertaking sustainable marketing projects and initiatives. Existing activity is, however, piecemeal and only touches the surface. Much more needs to be done, and city tourism organisation arguably should be to the fore as far as sustainable tourism is concerned, bearing in mind the tourist industry's deep-seated, inherent dependence on 'good' environment. By 2020, I trust that city tourism practitioners will have embraced 'full on' the sustainability agenda, so that they will be busy fulfilling their dreams in ways which permit future generations to fulfil theirs.

Finally, by 2012, city branding will at last have come of age! Existing initiatives such as 'I Amsterdam' demonstrate how city brands can be made to work so that the competitive advantages of a city are effectively promoted for the mutual benefit of all. In this way, the city brand refreshes the parts that 'sectoral' marketing campaigns addressing tourism, student, inward investor, property and resident audiences cannot reach. It is the 'umbrella' under which all of these separate campaigns can gain added value, and is the platform on which the resident community and its governance can 'talk up' their city. The 20 initiatives recorded in the first decade of the 20th century (refer Chapter 7) will doubtless have multiplied tenfold by 2020, and city branding will have become a mainstream instrument of urban policy.

So, that is city tourism and its organisation in 2020 from the vantage point of here and now: recovery in demand, but with lower annual growth rates; public–private partnership forms of city tourism organisation predominating; city tourism organisations that are 'fitter', financially more stable and rationalised, all of them carrying out 'bottom-up' web- and internet-based marketing rooted in social media and sustainability; and city branding as a mainstream tool of urban policy. That is how it might well pan out. But as the poet Robert Burns reminds us:

> *The best-laid schemes o' mice and men*
>
> *Gang aft agley.*

Roughly translated, this means that in practice things do not always work out as you expect them to!

References

AloA Consultancy (2009) The Hague City Marketing 2010–2020: Big talk in The Hague, or the linking element in improving The Hague's competitive position.

Amsterdam Partners (2008) *2008 Annual Report*.

Anholt, S. (2007) *Competitive Identity: The New Brand Management for Nations, Cities and Regions*. Basingstoke: Palgrave Macmillan.

Barcelona Tourism (June 2008) Turisme de Barcelona. PowerPoint presentation.

Berenschot (2003) *Choosing Amsterdam: Brand Concept and Organisation of the City Marketing*. Amsterdam: Berenschot.

Bjerkne, C. (June 2008) Gothenburg & Co. PowerPoint presentation. European Cities Marketing Annual Conference, Belgrade.

Black, J. (2003) *The British Abroad: The Grand Tour in the Eighteenth Century*. New Haven, CT: Yale University Press.

Braun, E. (2008) *City Marketing: Towards an Integrated Approach*. Rotterdam: Erasmus University.

Brown, F. (1998) *Tourism Reassessed: Blight or Blessing*? Oxford: Butterworth.

Bryson, B. (1991) *Neither Here Nor There: Travels in Europe*. London: Secker and Warburg.

Bryson, B. (1995) *Notes from a Small Island*. London: Doubleday.

City of Amsterdam (2004) The making of the city marketing of Amsterdam.

Clark, G. (2006) *City Marketing and Economic Development* (pp. 1–81). Paper submitted to the International City Marketing Summit. Madrid.

Coccossis, H. and Mexa, A. (eds) (2004) *The Challenge of Tourism Carrying Capacity Assessment*. Aldershot: Algate.

Davies, H. (1980) *William Wordsworth: A Biography*. London: Weidenfield and Nicholson.

de Botton, A. (2003) *The Art of Travel*. London: Penguin.

de Selincourt (ed.) (1981) *William Wordsworth: Guide to the Lakes*. Oxford: Oxford University Press.

Delgado, A. (1977) *The Annual Outing and Other Excursions*. London: Allen Unwin.

DK Eyewitness Travel Guides: Europe (2006) London: Dorling Kindersley.

Dominicus, H. (June 2004) New trends in finance of tourist boards in Europe 2004. PowerPoint presentation. European Cities Marketing annual conference, Nice.

Dublin Tourism (2007) *Annual Report 2006*.

Dublin Tourism (2007) *Making It Happen – Dublin Regional Tourism Plan 2008–2010*.

Duran, P. (2005) *The Impact of the Games on Tourism: Barcelona – the Legacy of the Games*. Barcelona: Centre for Olympic Studies.

Elborough, T. (2010) *Wish You Were Here: England on Sea*. London: Sceptre.

Elliott, J. (1997) *Tourism: Politics and Public Sector Management*. London: Routledge.

England: The Rough Guide (1994). London: Rough Guide Ltd.

European Cities Marketing (ECM) (2009) *The European Cities' Visitors Report – Special Edition.*

European Cities Marketing (ECM) (2010) *Benchmarking Report 2010.*

Flanagan, S. and Dunne, G. (2009) Dublin visitor survey. PowerPoint presentation. European Cities Marketing Spring Meeting, Dublin.

Friel, E.J. (1989) Convention market. In S.F. Witt and L. Moutinho (eds) *Tourism Marketing and Management Handbook*. Hemel Hempstead: Prentice-Hall.

Garrigosa, A. (2008) Case study of a leading convention bureau. PowerPoint presentation. European Cities Marketing Annual Conference, Belgrade.

Glasgow Marketing Bureau (2006) *Glasgow's Tourism Strategy to 2016.*

Glasgow Marketing Bureau (2007) *Glasgow: Scotland with Style: The City Brand*. The Bureau.

Gothenburg & Co. (2008) *The Company 2009.*

Gothenburg & Co. (2010) *Annual Report 2009.*

Hanna, V. (1992) *Communications in Birmingham: An Interim Report*. Viewpoint Group Ltd.

Hattersley, R. (1978) *Goodbye to Yorkshire* (p. 29). Harmondsworth: Penguin.

Heeley, J. (1975) A study of organisations concerned with tourism in the UK. MSc thesis, University of Strathclyde.

Heeley, J. (1980a) The definition of tourism in Great Britain: Does terminological confusion have to rule? *Tourist Review* 35, 11–14.

Heeley, J. (1980b) Tourism and local government, with special reference to the county of Norfolk. PhD thesis, University of East Anglia.

Heeley, J. (1986) A tale of two cities and tourism. *Fraser of Allander Institute Quarterly Economic Commentary* 11, 49–54.

Heeley, J. (1989) Heritage and tourism: An overview. *Heritage, Tourism and Leisure* (pp. 3–19). Glasgow: The Planning Exchange.

Heeley, J. (2001) Public–private sector partnerships in tourism. In A. Lockwood and S. Medlik (eds) *Tourism and Hospitality in the 21st Century* (pp. 273–283). Oxford: Butterworth Heinemann.

Heeley, J. and Pearlman, M. (1988) The Glasgow Garden Festival: Making Glasgow miles better? *Fraser of Allander Institute Quarterly Economic Commentary* 14, 65–70.

Johnston, S. (February 2009) Dublin card: Presentation to ECM City Cards Knowledge Group. PowerPoint presentation. European Cities Marketing Spring conference, Dublin.

Kotler, P. (1993) *Marketing Places: Attracting Investment, Industry and Tourism to Cities, States and Nations*. New York: Free Press.

Maastricht Region Branding Foundation (2009) *Working Together to Build a Strong Brand for the Maastricht Region* (p. 7). The Foundation, April 2009.

Maitland, R. and Ritchie, B. (2009) *City Tourism: National Capital Perspectives*. Wallingford: CABI Bookshop.

Marketing Birmingham (2002) *Our Birmingham Vision.*

McLuhan, M. (1964) *Understanding Media – The Extensions of Man*. London: Routledge and Kegan Paul.

McManus, R. (2001) Dublin's changing tourism geography. *Irish Geography* 34, 103–123.

Middleton, V.T.C. and Lickorish, L.J. (2005) *British Tourism: The Remarkable Story of Growth*. Oxford: Butterworth-Heinemann.

Morgan, N., Pritchard, A. and Pride, R. (eds) (2004) *Destination Branding: Creating the Unique Destination Branding*. Oxford: Butterworth Heinemann.

Morton, H.V. (1939) *In Search of England*. London: Methuen.

Neale, R.S. (1981) *Bath: A Social History 1680–1850 or a Valley of Pleasure, Yet a Sink of Iniquity*. London: Routledge and Kegan Paul.

Novotny, V. (2007) Prague Information Service. PowerPoint presentation European Cities Marketing Autumn Meeting Prague.

Olins, W. (2008) *The Brand Handbook*. London: Thames and Hudson.

Orwell, G. (1982) *Homage to Catalonia and Looking Back on the Spanish Civil War* (pp. 8–9). Harmondsworth: Penguin.

Pike, S. (2004) *Destination Marketing Organisations: Bridging Theory and Practice*. Oxford: Butterworth Heinemann.

Pike, S. (2008) *Destination Marketing: An Integrated Marketing Communications Approach*. Oxford: Butterworth Heinemann.

Pimlott, J.A.R. (1947) *The Englishman's Holiday: A Social History*. London: Faber & Faber.

Ponti, O. and Sager, C. (2009) Benchmarking European cities 2002–2007. Power Point presentation European Cities Marketing Spring Meeting, Dublin.

Priestley, J.B. (2009) *Journey through England*. Ilkley: Great Northern Books.

Sugrue, C. (2006) Case study Ireland. PowerPoint presentation. European Cities Marketing Autumn Meeting, Dubrovnic.

Uris, J. and Uris, L. (1984) *Ireland: A Terrible Beauty*. London: Corgi Books.

Vienna Tourist Board (2006) 50 years and the future 1955–2005.

Vienna Tourist Board (2010) Live life, enjoy creativity – International media coverage of Vienna in 2009.

Walton, J.K. (1983) *The English Seaside Resort: A Social History 1790–1914*. Leicester: Leicester University Press.

Weber, K. and Chon, K.S. (2002) *Convention Tourism: International Research and Industry Perspectives*. Binghampton, NY: The Haworth Press.

Weiss, B. (2009) Vienna.: PowerPoint presentation. First Lviv Tourism Conference.

Whitfield, G. (2008) Mountains don't smile back. *DMO World e-Newsletter.* Issue 2, January 2005.

Young, G. (1973) *Tourism: Blessing or Blight?* Harmondsworth: Penguin.

Index